Sex, Crime and Morality

Over the past few decades, there has been a marked increase in media and debate surrounding a specific group of offences in modern democratic nations that are labelled "crimes against morality". Included within this group are offences related to prostitution and pornography, homosexuality, and incest and child sexual abuse. This book examines the nexus between sex, crime and morality from a theoretical perspective.

This is the first academic text to offer an examination and analysis of the philosophical underpinnings of sex-related crimes and social attitudes towards them, and the historical, anthropological and moral reasons for differentiating these crimes in contemporary western culture.

The book is divided into three sections corresponding to three theoretical frameworks:

- Part 1 examines the moral temporality of sex and taboo as a foundation for legislation governing sex crimes.
- Part 2 focuses on the geography of sex and deviance, specifically notions of public morality and the public–private divide.
- Part 3 examines the moral economy of sex and harm, including the social construction of harm.

Sex, Crime and Morality will be key reading for students of criminology, criminal justice, gender studies and ethics, and will also be of interest to justice professionals.

Sharon Hayes is Senior Lecturer in Justice at Queensland University of Technology, Brisbane, Australia. Sharon has been researching and teaching in the areas of criminal justice, criminology and ethics for the past twenty years, and has published extensively in the areas of sexuality/gender studies, specifically sex and crime, same-sex domestic violence and sexuality in the classroom.

Belinda Carpenter is Professor in the School of Justice, in the Faculty of Law at Queensland University of Technology, Brisbane, Australia. She has published widely on the issue of prostitution, including the book: *Rethinking Prostitution: Feminism, Sex and the Self.* New York, Peter Lang (2000).

Angela Dwyer is Senior Lecturer in the School of Justice, in the Faculty of Law at Queensland University of Technology, Brisbane, Australia. Her research interests include sexuality and criminal justice, sex and crime, sex trafficking, prostitution, the body and criminality, young people and popular culture, and qualitative research methods.

Sex, Crime and Morality

*Sharon Hayes and Belinda Carpenter
with Angela Dwyer*

Routledge
Taylor & Francis Group

LONDON AND NEW YORK

First published 2012
by Routledge
2 Park Square, Milton Park, Abingdon, Oxon, OX14 4RN

Simultaneously published in the USA and Canada
by Routledge
711 Third Avenue, New York, NY 10017

Routledge is an imprint of the Taylor & Francis Group, an informa business

British Library Cataloguing in Publication Data
A catalogue record for this book is available from the British Library

Library of Congress Cataloging-in-Publication Data
Hayes, Sharon.
Sex, crime and morality / by Sharon Hayes, Belinda Carpenter with
Angela Dwyer.
p. cm.
ISBN 978-1-84392-816-4 (hardback) – ISBN 978-1-84392-815-7 (pbk.) –
ISBN 978-0-203-15373-4 (ebk.) 1. Sex crimes–Moral and ethical aspects.
I. Carpenter, Belinda J., 1963- II. Dwyer, Angela. III. Title.
HV6556.H39 2012
364.15′3–dc23
2011022967

ISBN: 978-1-84392-816-4 hbk
ISBN: 978-1-84392-815-7 pbk
ISBN: 978-0-203-15373-4 ebk

Typeset in Bembo
by Taylor & Francis Books

Printed and bound in Great Britain by
TJ International Ltd, Padstow, Cornwall

Contents

Acknowledgments

Many people gave of their time and support during the writing of this book, and we would like to acknowledge and thank them for their assistance. In particular, we thank Professor The Hon. Michael Lavarch and the Faculty of Law, Queensland University of Technology, for supporting this project with professional development leave funding, and Professor Kerry Carrington, Head of the School of Justice at QUT, for allowing us this time to write, as well as for her ongoing encouragement and advice. The School of Communication, Cultural Studies and Media at Nottingham Trent University was kind enough to provide space, support and a rich scholarly environment for Sharon during writing, and the arguments in this book benefited greatly from discussions with Liz Morrish, Louise Cummings, Gary Needham and other members of the school. Feedback from students of the Master of Criminology seminar at Loughborough University was also enormously helpful. Chris Holt, of Federation Press, was generous of his time and feedback in the early stages, which we very much appreciated. Thanks also to Julia Willan for her editorial support and for processing the manuscript so quickly into production. We'd also like to thank colleagues at QUT, especially Gordon Tait and Matthew Ball, for the many theoretical and practical discussions that fed the development of our thesis. Finally, we owe a huge debt of gratitude to our families, partners and children, without whose encouragement and support we would never have finished.

1

INTRODUCTION

Recently, we were fortunate enough to attend a seminar on sex work and sex blogging, listening to a paper by Kitty Stryker, sometime postgraduate student, full-time sex worker/blogger and self-proclaimed dominatrix.[1] While sex, crime and morality has been a topic of research interest for us for some time now, we didn't fully understand the impact of the connection until we were sitting watching ten-foot-high images of bondage scenes flash across the screen as Kitty delivered her speech. In her dulcet Californian accent, she described how men and women would seek her out, engage her services and pay her for them. She was, she claimed, not your average dominatrix – no cat suit and spiked heels for Kitty, it seemed. It was all converse sneakers, ponytails and geeky glasses, though she clearly had the curvaceous equipment one usually thinks of when picturing the image of your stereotypical dominatrix. What was interesting, though – apart from the incongruous geekiness – was her feminist understanding of her trade. She might whip people in tender places, tie them to the bed and make them submit – and enjoy it – but she was damned if she was going to compromise her feminist identity for the sake of some sick misogynist fantasy about thigh-high boots and leather! What this brought home to us was just how far we, as a society, have come in terms of conceptualizing and talking about sex in general, and sex work in particular. Chapter 7 of this book gives a more detailed description and analysis of that seminar, but here we just want to point out the way in which, as Jeffrey Weeks puts it, we are constantly participating in the "remaking of erotic and intimate life".[2]

As recently as the 1980s, feminists were arguing that sex work and pornography damaged women beyond repair,[3] religious groups were campaigning against all kinds of things to do with sex, and the general public kept sex talk pretty much under its hat, the combination of which drove sexual commerce underground and resulted in a new Puritanism that lasted almost into the twenty-first century. There has been a shift, however, in how we think and talk about sex, and in what we find acceptable.

Western nations particularly have been repealing legislation regulating sexuality and sex work, and the topic of sex has suddenly become acceptable, not only in academic and intellectual circles. Sitting in the seminar, we couldn't help but marvel at this shift in perspective, even as a fundamentalist Islamic student group gathered outside our seminar room for their weekly meeting. The incongruousness of these two groups coexisting signifies just how much broader we, as a society, view the bounds of acceptable practices. Weeks comments that this can be attributed to "the global circulation of the idea of non-heterosexual, non-familial choice"[4] in sex as something to which more and more individuals are subscribing. This book takes that observation as its starting point.

Concomitant to this shift, however, we have also seen a massive increase in the legislation and regulation of other forms of non-normative sexual behaviour. At no other time in history has incest and child sexual abuse, for example, been more publicly reviled. Similarly, sex trafficking has come under fire, particularly in the United States and the UK. Both have created what we often hear described as "moral panics", fuelled by both media and political attention, creating a perception in society that sexual predators are everywhere and that our children are no longer safe. The nexus between sex, crime and morality, then, is complex and multilayered, and grounded in conflicting social perceptions and discourses. We hope this book unravels some of this complexity and provides insight into how sex, crime and morality interact in our society.

The germination of this book occurred over several years after two of us were asked to write a chapter for a criminology textbook. The topic was to be "crimes against morality" and, initially, we conceived of such crimes as those we sometimes refer to as "victimless crimes". After several brainstorming sessions and a couple of bouts of procrastination, we discovered that our perceptions weren't quite right – that, in fact, the very naming of a crime as victimless was problematic, fraught with complexities from a variety of standpoints, including (but not confined to) feminism, psychology, public health and criminology itself. The idea that a behaviour or action entered into by informed adults (and which does not harm others) should be criminalized seems paternalistic at best, and yet it is clear that morality and moral values underpin so many of our laws – so, why not these ones? On the other hand, there is some doubt about whether crimes such as prostitution and recreational drug use are actually victimless. Unless an individual acts in complete isolation, their actions exponentially affect a number of others, depending on the social, legal and personal relationships with which they engage. To make things more complicated, we realized that the kinds of crimes that raise the most public debate concerning criminalization were those that had something to do with sex. While decriminalization of recreational drug use has been raised a number of times in public arenas over the past three decades, these are not the kinds of crimes that tend to create moral panic – rather, it was crimes such as child sexual abuse, sex work and pornography that raised levels of public ire on a regular basis, and that were the cause of spirited exchanges in both media and parliament. Thus began our ongoing debate, through which we slowly came to realize that most "crimes against morality" had less to do with being victimless and much more to do with values and beliefs about sex, sexuality and the family.

The purpose of this book, then, is to examine the nexus between sex, crime and morality. We take a multidisciplinary perspective because we want to explore a variety of discourses from legal, criminological, philosophical, feminist and psychological perspectives. While we will argue that all crimes have a general moral basis, condemned as "wrong" or "bad" in the society in which they are proscribed, the specific group of offences in modern democratic nations that bear the brunt of the label include prostitution, sex trafficking and pornography, homosexuality, and incest and child sexual abuse. Interestingly, the offences of incest and child sexual abuse are differentiated legally (if not morally) from sex crimes such as rape and sexual assault. This book examines the historical, anthropological and moral reasons for such differentiations in contemporary western culture. We will not, however, examine rape and sexual assault *per se*. This book is not about violence and violent crimes; rather, it is about those sex crimes that are not necessarily already covered by the criminal code in terms of assault and bodily harm.

What these crimes have in common, apart from a sexual basis, is that there is some debate over whether they result in sexual harm, in both a moral and a psychological sense, as well as physically. Conversely, they *are* often argued to be victimless crimes, especially when the acts occur between consenting adults. Finally, they are considered essentially private acts, but they often occur and are regulated in the public domain. Most importantly, each of these crimes against morality has only relatively recently (that is, in the past 150 years) become identified and regulated by the state as a criminal offence.

These crimes now take up a large part of the public, political and cultural agenda. Over the past few decades, there have been debates over the legitimacy and status of same-sex relationships, the legality or illegality of prostitution, the role of pornography in consenting adult relationships, and the problem of child sexual abuse. These debates have occurred in both Australia and the UK, and across the rest of the western world. They have culminated in a range of political and legislative responses, including the decriminalization of brothel prostitution in many parts of the west, often combined with a concomitant increase in the penalties against other forms of commercial sex, such as street prostitution; a relaxation in the laws concerning same-sex partnerships and homosexuality across Australia, UK, parts of the USA and Europe; an explosion in the amount of pornography available via the world wide web and a range of approaches to its production and policing; an increasingly hard-line approach to all forms of child sexual abuse; and a heavily punitive regime of penalties aimed at sex offenders.

While the places where sex and morality meet have shifted over time, these two concepts continue to form the basis of criminal legislation. Such offenders of sexual mores are positioned as the reviled corruptors of innocent children, the purveyors of disease, an indictment on the breakdown of the family and/or the secularization of society, and a corruptive force. While other types of offending may divide public and political opinion, the consensus on sex crimes appears constant. This book examines the origins of these attitudes and offers a reinterpretation of the traditional approach to crimes such as prostitution, pornography, incest and homosexuality through a re-examination of a range of philosophical concepts, including harm, consent, freedom and victimization. We hope this book offers a unique analysis of the theoretical underpinnings of sex-related crimes and the social attitudes towards them.

The book is divided into three sections corresponding to three theoretical frameworks: Part 1 examines legal moralism and legal paternalism as a foundation for legislation governing sex crimes; Part 2 focuses on the notion of a public morality and the public–private divide as a way of understanding how sex crimes are categorized and regulated; and Part 3 examines the social construction of harm in order to highlight the connection between sex, consent and social mores. In each section, two case studies of sex crimes are used to illustrate the particular theoretical concepts, which are reworked for a contemporary audience. We wish to note that the choice of case studies is purely for illustration purposes – each of the sex crimes discussed in each section of the book could just as easily be examined within either of the other two theoretical frameworks. For example, in Part 1 we chose incest and pornography to illustrate the moral temporality of sex and taboo. However, both these crimes fit just as easily into a discussion about the moral geography of sex and crime (discussed in Part 2) or the moral economy of sex and harm (Part 3). The rationale for choosing the case studies in each section was informed by the context in which those crimes are generally thought about. Social perceptions about the dangers of pornography and incest have developed in fascinating ways over the past several centuries, and these crimes seemed the perfect illustration in the context of a discussion about moral temporality. Similar rationales, of course, also characterize Parts 2 and 3. We have endeavoured to make the rationale in each section of the book as clear as possible, and hope this will enable the reader to engage with the theoretical framework in ways that are meaningful to them.

As mentioned above, Part 1 discusses the relationship between law and morality. Morality does not necessarily coincide with the law, but it contributes to it. An act may be legal, but nevertheless considered to be immoral in a particular society. For example, the use of pornography may be considered by many to be immoral. Nevertheless, the sale and distribution of non-violent, non-child-related, sexually explicit material is legal (or regulated) in many jurisdictions. Many laws are informed by, and even created by, morality. Part 1 thus examines the historical influence of morality on the law and on society in general. Chapter 2 aims to develop a theoretical framework for examining legal moralism and the social construction of morality and crime, as well as the relationship between sex, desire and taboo. Here, we refer to the moral temporality of sex and taboo, which examines the way in which moral judgments about sex and what is considered taboo change over time, and the kinds of justifications that are employed in support of changing moralities. It unpacks the way in which abstract and highly tenuous concepts such as "desire", "art" and "entertainment" may be "out of time" with morality, and how morality shapes laws over time, fabricating justifications from within socially constructed communities of practice. This theoretical framework maps the way in which these concepts have become temporally dominated by *heteronormative* structures such as the family, marriage, reproduction and longevity. In this context, heteronormativity refers to the normalizing of heterosexual structures and relationships, and the marginalization of everything that doesn't conform. We argue that the logic of these structures is inexorably tied to the heterosexual life-path, charting individual lives and relationships through explicit phases of childhood, adolescence and adulthood that, in the twenty-first century, delimit the boundaries of taboo surrounding sex more than at any other time in history.

In chapter 3, we argue that morality and taboo come together in the modern psyche over a concern with incest and sexual relations between related family members. The conceptualization and identification of incest as a sex crime is relatively new and is based upon recent ideas about the innocence and asexuality of children, the predatory nature of men, and the harm and damage to the victim caused by such abuse. We discuss cases such as Josef and Elisabeth Fritzl, which recently made media headlines, with a view to explaining why this case attracted such horror and outrage, and argue that it is contemporary understandings of childhood that have had the most impact on current views about the moral taboo of incest. Such a shift in our moral understanding of children underpins the fear for the child as a sexual victim, and has led to the defining of father/daughter incest as *the* harm to which children are at risk. Incest, however, has a long and varied history. Our modern understanding has enabled incest to be named, perpetrators to be punished, and victims to be treated. However, this new incarnation of the moral taboo of incest is the culmination of 150 years of social and legal concerns over children and sex. Certainly such acts are harmful and abhorrent in the context of the twenty-first century, but the belief that a large proportion of the population is at risk of such harm is misleading. Such a focus on the harm of sex for children under the age of sixteen also ignores the fact that, within the criminal justice system, children as young as thirteen years of age are held to be capable of reason and intent. This differentiation between criminal responsibility and sexual responsibility highlights both the arbitrary nature of the age of consent and the clear boundary between sexual knowledge and childhood.

Chapter 4 charts key discursive shifts that have led to modern ways of thinking about pornography as a morally contentious issue. By charting the historical relation between pornography and obscenity, we will discuss the shift from a public discourse of sex, where sex formed a prominent part of much reading material, and was consumed as part of the public discussion of sexual matters, to the private consumption of pornography, which was created as sexually explicit material specifically designed to elicit a sexual response. Moreover, we will explore how this shift from sex as a public discourse to sex as a private discourse was accompanied by larger shifts in the regulation of sexuality, especially for women and children, and chart how this shift can be traced, in part, to a significant change in the way in which male and female sexuality was understood at this time. Most specifically, the nineteenth-century discovery of the irrelevance of an orgasm for women in the process of conception severed the link between pleasure and sex that had much to do with changing notions of femininity as passive and asexual. This has had major implications for the ways in which pornography is currently conceptualized. Finally, we will discuss how current perceptions of sexual development, which, as we have seen in chapters 2 and 3, draw heavily on notions of sexual innocence and sexual purity, have been shaped historically by moral concerns about children and sex, which came to the fore in concerns about masturbation, or solitary sex, linked specifically to the rise of visual pornography. The shift from literary to visual pornography was the moment when regulation was required to manage the working class and children, who, it was maintained, did not have the competencies to consume sexually explicit material.

Part 2 examines the nexus between crime, morality and public space, and questions whether we can identify a public morality. We all subscribe to certain social norms and conventions that suggest that, as a society, we share some common values. However, there is some debate about what those values are and what they mean. This section explores the idea of a public morality and the divide between public and private morality. It also examines the concept of offensive behaviour and the social construction of what is offensive, and traces the development of legislation governing public indecency in the UK and Australia. As such, it analyses the moral geography of sex and crime, specifically, how public space is used to regulate certain acts. This is illustrated by two case studies – the regulation of child sex offenders and sexually non-normative individuals – to describe how conceptions of the public and private have developed and influenced what is acceptable behaviour in public and private spaces. In chapter 5, we explore the theoretical underpinnings of moral geography and how public space directs the criminalization of certain sex acts, and the governing of criminals associated with these acts. The chapter traces the historical development of the notion of space and unpacks the rationale behind how spaces at large are governed, particularly with respect to sexual behaviour. We argue that, because of the heteronormative nature of public morality, which privileges traditional institutions such as families and heterosexual marriage, public spaces are governed by legislation preventing individuals from engaging in acts that are considered offensive to those ideals.

In chapter 6, we examine social and legal discourses concerning child sex offenders and how they are governed. Contemporary ideas about sex offenders have emerged primarily out of understandings of dangerousness and immutability. This chapter examines public perceptions of sex offenders as perverted and therefore inherently immoral persons. While historical contexts demonstrate that sex offenders were always a key social problem for ecclesiastical and criminal justice authorities, such offenders were usually regarded as simply perverted – not as dangerous predators. Thus we explore how the later emergence of the "sexual psychopath" as a psychological and medical category has as its corollary the need for children to be safeguarded at all times. Insisting that sex offenders are morally perverted *and* dangerous predators serves to appease the community at large, who demand government protection of private spaces reserved for heterosexual families.

Chapter 7 examines discourses about sex and sexuality, and continues to explore the concept of moral space with particular reference to "deviant" sexualities. As noted above, public discourses about sex have changed remarkably over recent years, and this chapter analyses the ways in which public discourses and public spaces have opened up to other sexualities in ways that appear quite liberating for the non-heterosexual. Indeed, the effects of such public discourses have been largely positive with respect to adult entertainment and other forms of sexual commerce, and we will be analysing those effects in chapters 9 and 10. In chapter 7, we focus on the effects of public discourses on sexual identity, and how the apparent opening up of public spaces and public discourses has actually contributed to the continued marginalization of sexual minorities.

Part 3 explores the nexus between sex, morality and harm through case studies on sexual commerce and sex trafficking. Chapter 8 develops a theoretical framework for this task by exploring the moral economy of sex and harm. A large proportion of what is considered sex harm is governed through the market, and sex work may or may not be considered harmful according to which discourses we are considering, which consumers it targets, and which markets govern it. We differentiate "moral sensibilities" from other kinds of harm, and examine the extent to which harm is situational or intrinsic. We also suggest that social discourses make a fatal mistake in attributing intrinsic harm to such activities as prostitution, adult entertainment, and even sex trafficking, arguing that it is not sexual commerce or migration *per se* that is harmful. Rather, it is pathological, systemic inequalities and entrenched disadvantage that is harmful, and harm in these contexts is expressed in the way inequality and disadvantage are played out through sexual commerce and intimate relationships.

Chapter 9 argues that sexual commerce has become a complex, multi-billion-dollar industry, both produced by, and itself driving, global developments in a vast array of other industries, including resorts and hotels, communication companies, entertainment industries, and computer and information technologies. This chapter examines the ways in which harm is understood to be an integral part of these encounters precisely because they involve sex in exchange for money. This dominant discourse began with the rise of first-wave feminism in the nineteenth century, and has since been the impetus for legislative and policy changes around the harm of prostitution. We question the relevance of laws about the public nuisance of prostitution and arguments about the inherent exploitation of sexual commerce, and hope to offer some insights into the changing nature of both sexual commerce and sexual relations more generally in the twenty-first century.

Chapter 10 extends the discussion about the inherent harm of sexual commerce by examining feminist historical understandings of sex trafficking that tend to collapse trafficking into prostitution. We argue that people move from poor countries to wealthy ones for all sorts of work, and that such migration has a long history. We also draw on discussions of harm discourse through history, tracking the collapse of trafficking to sex trafficking and prostitution through the discovery of the white slave trade by feminists and other moral reformers in the nineteenth century, through to the rediscovery of the harm discourse/moral panic around sex trafficking by modern feminists in the 1990s. These discourses have had extensive effects in terms of international policy on sex trafficking, which links illegality with vulnerability and coercion, as well as organized crime and terrorism. Discourses of slavery, bondage and imprisonment, especially concerning underage women and children, create a picture of the ultimate victim.

We endorse recent attempts at rethinking the concept through shifts in understanding sex trafficking from coercion to migration, a move that is supported by recent changes to United Nations definitions of the harm of trafficking.

We conclude our discussions of sex crimes in chapter 11 by summarizing the theoretical and methodological challenges we have issued throughout the book, and suggesting new ways of thinking about crime, sex and morality with a view to creating some impetus for developing different ways of regulating these crimes. It is hoped that both academics and non-academics will find some worth in the content hereafter, and so we follow Laura Maria Agustin, who, in her excellent book, *Sex at the Margins*,[5] had the foresight to replace "the insistent citation behaviour" required by academics with footnotes. References are thus supplied in endnotes at the end of the book so as not to interrupt the flow of words throughout.

Part 1

2

OUT OF TIME

The moral temporality of sex and taboo

Introduction

In 2008, an exhibition of photographic work in a prestigious gallery in Sydney, Australia, was raided by police and subsequently closed for public viewing. According to media reports of the time, the exhibition was closed because it consisted of images of "naked children as young as twelve in a variety of poses". The New South Wales Minister of Community Services sanctioned the raid on the premises, stating that the photographs were "highly inappropriate ... I can't see any reason why images of naked children need to be created or displayed in that way ... as a community, it's our responsibility to protect the innocence of childhood and these images step over the line".[1] The Australian Prime Minister, Kevin Rudd, defended the actions of the state government and police, describing the images as "revolting".[2] Such a position was supported by the Director of local child protection community group Bravehearts, who was concerned that the photographer seemed to have "an obsession with pre-teen nudity ... which is porn". Detectives also found a website depicting forty-one of the same naked images included in the exhibition, and these were swiftly removed, even though the website was hosted outside Australia and therefore beyond their jurisdiction.

What is most interesting about this case of alleged child pornography is that the photographer in question, Bill Henson, is a respected artist whose industrial landscapes and soulful images of androgynous young people have been acclaimed throughout the world for almost thirty years. In 2004, his work was lauded by *The New Yorker*, which stated that "his elegant, formal photographs ... of battered landscapes and fragile, wispy youths ... resemble nothing so much as Flemish still-lifes; rarely has colour photography captured so profoundly the furry texture of night time".

A year earlier, *Pavement* magazine[3] described Henson's photographs as "ambiguous spaces of adolescence" depicting "androgynous girls and boys adrift in the nocturnal turmoil of adolescence[, creating] painterly tableaux that continue the tradition of romantic literature and painting in our post-industrial age". To the art world, Henson is a shining light, a "photographer of the human condition and an experimenter of remarkable skill and conviction". Indeed, the fame and esteem in which he is held is not new. A glance at Henson's online profile[4] reveals that his work has been exhibited in some of the most prestigious galleries around the world, from Sydney to Paris, Rotterdam to New York and Tel Aviv. In 1990, it was the Bibliothèque Nationale in France; in 1991, the Circulo de Bellas Artes, Madrid, and so on. The Art Gallery of New South Wales presented Henson's work as a key element of the influential Sydney Festival in 2005 and the Gallery of Modern Art also displayed his work in Brisbane in 2007. Yet it has been argued that these images, which are lauded in artistic circles, can be classified as pornography under a variety of state laws.

This section explores the moral temporality of sex and taboo; that is, the way in which moral judgments about sex and what is considered taboo change over time, and the kinds of justifications that are employed in support of these changing moralities. It unpacks the way in which abstract and highly tenuous concepts such as "desire", "art" and "entertainment" may be "out of time" with morality, and how morality shapes laws over time, fabricating justifications from within socially constructed communities of practice that are tenuous almost to the point where they defy definition. We map the way in which, by normalizing heterosexual structures and relationships and marginalizing anything that doesn't conform, these concepts have become temporally dominated by heteronormative structures such as the family, marriage, reproduction and longevity. The logic of these structures, it will be demonstrated, is inexorably tied to the heterosexual life-path, charting individual lives and relationships through explicit phases of childhood, adolescence and adulthood that, in the twenty-first century, delimit the boundaries of taboo surrounding sex more than at any other time in history.

In order to interrogate the way in which notions such as desire and taboo are understood within the logic of heteronormative structures, three dimensions of moral temporality are examined. The first concerns the temporality of sexuality, that is, norms and beliefs about sexuality and sexual development and how these change over time. The second dimension involves the temporality of moral authority, or the way in which morality shifts to endorse or sanction sexuality and relationships. The third relates to the temporality of bodies and how they function as codifiers and markers of sexual normality and responsibility.

The temporality of sexual development

In the post-industrial age, the way we think about sex is framed by time and space. For any era, sexuality exists as a moment in time, and in our era, that moment is informed by heteronormative temporalities such as birth, childhood, puberty, adolescence, marriage, procreation, family and death.[5] Lives are scripted chronologically through what Judith Halberstam[6] terms the "logic of location, movement and identification" associated with familial and procreative dominance. This heteronormative temporality is identified by several important markers, including the prolonged extension and sacredization of childhood, and the ritual transition to adulthood through pubescence and adolescence.

The temporality of childhood has extended considerably over the past several centuries, at least in western industrialized countries. According to historians such as Phillipe Aries,[7] childhood came to be regarded as a distinct developmental phase only in the sixteenth century. Prior to that, children were regarded as small adults. Newman and Smith[8] note that depictions of children in art during that period generally characterized children as "shrunken replicas of their parents", with similar bodily proportions and dress. Children were also expected to act like adults, minding their manners, doing their fair share of work in the family, and generally acting independently in many ways.

> The notion that children deserve special protection and treatment did not exist at this time. Children could be punished, and frequently were, for social transgressions with the same severity that adults were.[9]

It has been suggested that this treatment of children was based on economic and social necessity. Infant and child mortality rates were high at this time, with plagues and diseases of all varieties running rampant in Europe. Emotional attachment to children wasn't a viable option, and parents tended to have as many children as possible to "hedge their bets".[10] The idea that children were vulnerable and needed protection didn't become popular until much later; indeed, child labour was extensive in the latter half of the eighteenth and first half of the nineteenth centuries.

It wasn't until industrialization took a firm hold, making child labour an anachronism, that children began to be seen as objects of affection and care, rather than as objects of labour and economic benefit. People began having children for personal satisfaction, and by the twentieth century, childhood had become a time in which children were nurtured and loved for themselves, rather than for what they could return economically.[11] At the same time, children came to be seen as completely different from adults, as innocent and essentially uncorrupted. Children became something to be cherished and protected from harm in order to grow and develop into responsible and productive adults. The emotional and intellectual naivete of children was recognized as central to this attitude, and by the latter decades of the twentieth century, children had achieved a status of vulnerability unrivalled in any other era.

This notion of the child as susceptible extends beyond mere physical protection to encompass sexual vulnerability as well. The heteronormative governing of families and individuals depends in part upon the capacity of the family and other institutions to keep children naive. Children are stripped of their sexuality to such an extent that they have become altogether asexual. Indeed, the association of sex with children is regarded as obscene, dangerous and taboo. Children are viewed as incapable of understanding and consenting to sexual activity, and so are removed from sexuality altogether. Adolescence came into being as a way of extending and sacredizing childhood. The construction of adolescence as a transitional period has extended, over the past several decades, to later and later ages. In the 1970s, for example, it was common for young people in Australia to leave school and seek paid work at age fifteen. Only a select few stayed on to finish high school and even fewer moved into tertiary education. By the 1990s, however, almost all young people were completing year 12 at high school and an increasing number were moving on to higher education.[12]

There are several related reasons for this extension of adolescence. The exponential development of technology has meant that young people are required to have higher levels of education than ever before in order to be able to participate in the workforce. It also means that young people are offered more opportunities for travel and other educational experiences that extend their knowledge and understanding of how the world works. Work and occupations have taken on much more formality over the past two decades, with the burgeoning of technical and further education colleges providing courses for almost every imaginable occupation, including even lower-level employment such as retail assistance and hospitality – occupations that were previously learned on the job.[13] The construction of adolescence as a transitional period has therefore been extended to coexist with the period of compulsory and higher education. The increased intellectualization of occupations has created a market for itself, making it difficult for young people to compete in the job market unless they have the relevant "qualifications", requiring more and more that they move into post-compulsory education and further delay their entry into the workforce and adulthood.[14]

This extension of adolescence into the third decade of life is accompanied by a reconfiguring of sex and sexuality for young people in that generation. Whereas in previous centuries, young women often married in their teens, today they are expected to get an education and move into the workforce before committing to a life partnership and children. Sex and sexuality, then, have become topics of controversy, especially concerning the age at which a young person is considered mature enough to engage in a sexual relationship. In most western countries, the age of consent has been set at sixteen for heterosexual intercourse and between sixteen and eighteen for homosexual anal intercourse,[15] based upon perceptions of young people's capacity to make an informed choice about entering into sexual activity. But these temporal delineations are not meant to apply to sexual activity between young people of the same age. Sexual activity between children and between adolescents may be frowned upon, and considered precocious, but it is not criminalized.[16] Sex between the "underaged", while the subject of much preventive activity (in the form of sex education and institutionalized moral sanctions), is seen as folly, excusable and even understandable. Young people are "risk-takers" who cannot be held accountable for their actions and must therefore be objects of paternalistic intervention.[17]

On the other hand, sex between the underaged and adults is taboo of the highest order. Sex between children (of relatively similar age) is acceptable because it is regarded as an innocent exploration, possibly based on a lack of knowledge and understanding, and focused on curiosity and sheer desire. Sex between adults and children is seen as a power imbalance that necessarily disadvantages and exploits the child. The younger participant is regarded as incapable of reasonably consenting to the interaction, and is therefore vulnerable, a victim. The older, adult participant is seen as wielding all the power in the interaction and is therefore cast as predator.[18] It is unclear, however, whether this construction of adult/child sex is borne out in everyday life. A recent case study illuminates the possible tensions underlying these assumptions.

In 1997 in the USA, a female high school teacher, Mary Kay Letourneau, was convicted of child sexual abuse for having an affair with her then thirteen-year-old male student, Vili Fualaau.[19] Newspaper articles at the time report that Letourneau first came into contact with Fualaau in second grade. Their affair began when he was in sixth grade and twelve years old. As student and teacher they became very close over the years, and by sixth grade, Fualaau was spending time at his teacher's home, socializing with her then husband and their three children. The pair first had sexual intercourse in the same grade, when Fualaau was thirteen and Letourneau thirty-four. Their relationship was discovered when they were caught having sex in her car. The teacher was convicted of second-degree statutory rape and sent to prison for seven and a half years, all but six months of that suspended. She was required to agree never to see Fualaau again and to participate in a three-year-long rehabilitation programme. However, after Letourneau was released from her six-month prison stint, she again struck up a relationship with Fualaau and, when discovered, was sent back to prison to serve the remainder of her original sentence. She gave birth to their child while in prison. Fualaau was nineteen when she was finally freed and he immediately signed a release so that Letourneau was no longer required to keep her distance. They married when Letourneau was forty-three and Fualaau was twenty-two, and at the time of writing have two children.

Fualaau has consistently denied being coerced into the relationship. He claimed that he went through puberty at age ten and was both sexually and emotionally capable of entering into a relationship with his teacher at age twelve. The issue of whether a thirteen-year-old is capable of giving informed consent is a difficult one. Consent is differentially defined temporally and geographically. In some jurisdictions in Japan and in Spain, for example, the age of consent is thirteen.[20] Clearly, Japanese and Spanish adolescents are considered capable of giving informed consent, whereas American (not to mention British and Australian) teenagers are not. This difference in cultural values and beliefs about sex gives us some indication of the relative arbitrariness of the age-lines drawn between childhood and adulthood, especially where sexual activity across generations is concerned.

Another issue in the Letourneau/Fualaau case is the teacher–student relationship. Teachers are regarded as having a duty of care toward their students, which requires them to prevent harm to their students wherever possible. Article 19 of the United Nations *Convention on the Rights of the Child* states that children (defined as people under eighteen) must be protected "from all forms of physical or mental violence, injury or abuse, neglect or negligent treatment, maltreatment or exploitation, including sexual abuse, while in the care of parent(s), legal guardian(s) or any other person who has the care of the child".[21] The question, then, is whether sexual activity between a teacher and student (regardless of age) can be considered "abuse". The law in most western countries states that it is.[22] Certainly, from this perspective,

Letourneau was delinquent in her duty of care to her student by forming a personal relationship with him – sexual or not.

At the same time as children's sexuality has been obliterated and sexual activity with children criminalized, they have also become sexualized in ways that contradict the assumptions underlying criminalization. The production and marketing of consumer goods aimed at children, especially clothing, music, dance and cinema, have sexualized children's bodies, especially girls. Dressed as imitation adults, and engaged in a highly sexualized popular culture, children's bodies function as objects of desire while at the same time being objects of taboo. Young girls dress in revealing, sexy outfits meant to flatter and entice, and yet adults are meant to turn a blind eye to their overt seductiveness. When nubile young women reach puberty, this tension becomes even more pronounced, since now these young girls have adult bodies, and the blurring of the line between child and adult becomes disturbing. Indeed, we suggest that it is the sexualization of young women, and the accompanying tension that results, that strengthens the taboo on adult/adolescent sex. Pubescent young people are suggestive of sex and all that it accompanies, and must therefore be protected from it at all costs.

This tension between desire and taboo creates an undercurrent of distrust concerning the display of naked young bodies. The naked and semi-naked young people depicted in Henson's photographs are suggestive. They speak to the sexual potential of young people as well as to the perceived inability of adults to regard naked young bodies as anything but sexual. That adults may recognize the artistic quality of such photographs is discounted as a mask for what is regarded essentially as a burgeoning and uncontrollable desire that characterizes all adults. The adult gaze can look upon a naked body only with desire, regardless of the context. Children must therefore be protected from the adult gaze, for what the adult sees, it covets, and is in danger of appropriating. Children are seen as powerless and unwilling objects of this adult desire and appropriation. Thus the condemnation of Henson's work is based on three assumptions – that children are naive and sexually vulnerable; that adults always desire naked bodies, regardless of age, sex or context; and that adults cannot be trusted to contain that desire. The resulting legal moralism that criminalizes sex between adults and children is designed to ensure that adult desire is controlled and sanctioned where necessary, and that children will remain innocent of sex and sexuality for as long as possible.

Accompanying and reinforcing the legal moralism surrounding sexual relationships is the belief that adult sex is somehow "dirty" or wrong unless it is performed for the purpose of procreation, or tied to marriage and families, and thereby to respectability and normality. Only procreative sex or sex within the confines of marriage is pure and therefore acceptable. But even then, sex must be kept hidden from children, lest it corrupt them. Thus even pure expressions of procreative, intra-marital sex are taboo where children are concerned. Sex must never be performed in public. Sex and sexuality must therefore be kept behind closed doors. Legal moralism polices the connection between sex and procreation/family, and between sex and public spaces. Moral attitudes to sex in public spaces are examined in Part 2, but it is important here to understand the reach of legal moralism as encompassing not just sexual and developmental timelines, but also the geography of sex and sexuality.

It is in this context that Henson's youth are seen as corrupted or wronged. Their innocent young naked bodies have been exposed to sex and desire "out of time". The art world sees Henson's images of naked children not as objects, but as subjects – the frail, haunting subjects of a postmodern era – but the objectification of bodies, especially naked bodies, is so entrenched that the artistic gaze is reinterpreted by the non-artist, constructed as uncontainable desire, and condemned. The assumption that adults are always at risk of acting on their desire means that every adult is guilty until proven innocent. We cannot trust adults to keep their desires in check. Children's bodies must therefore be kept hidden, and children themselves must be safeguarded.

The temporality of moral authority

The extension of childhood into a longer and longer timeframe ensures that moral values surrounding sex and sexuality are upheld, and that transgressions are sanctioned. Young people who attempt to subvert the moral boundaries encompassing their generation by being sexually precocious are punished, either directly or indirectly, through the criminal justice system (for example, in cases of illegal intergenerational sex), or through social ostracism and vilification (for example, in cases of legal but socially unacceptable explorations of sexuality between similar-aged youth).

This also speaks to a perceived need to control young people, who are otherwise exposed to a variety of dangerous temptations and opportunities to resist normality and respectability. Legal moralism ensures that young people, and those who would be wrongfully involved with them, are disciplined in timely and appropriate ways, much as Mary Jane Letourneau and Vili Fualaau were disciplined for openly defying the taboo on adult–child sex. However, the disciplining of young people extends beyond sex and sexuality to include almost all areas of life. The capital abundance that characterizes much of western civilization means that young people are able to buy a greater variety of goods and services, including sexy clothes and music; but such access to capital also encompasses advanced technology that temporally and geographically extends the experience of young people beyond the scope of local disciplinary reach. Reproductive technologies mean that they can no longer be disciplined and held in check by the threat of pregnancy and sexually transmitted infections. Electronic and internet technologies mean that they can no longer be prevented from accessing morally questionable material or from participating in unsavoury and dangerous virtual relationships. This seemingly inevitable exposure to morally questionable activities is governed by a variety of legally and morally imposed limits, many of which are policed purely by the panoptic fear of discovery and disapproval, rather than any real legal power. Children are made very aware of what adults expect of them, and therefore are on alert for disapproval and disenfranchisement.

Tied into this view of the potential waywardness of young people is the technology of child-rearing, which has become a burgeoning body of knowledge in disciplines as diverse as medicine, psychiatry, social sciences and philosophy. Child-rearing theories and practices, while as disparate as the disciplines from which they emerge, nevertheless are united in their support of the logic of safety. Children are potential citizens and must be trained and nurtured in ways that benefit the citizenry as a whole. But they are also at risk, both from unscrupulous adults and older youth, and from their own risky behaviour. The logic of safety requires that adult carers take on board potential dangers and work to prevent exposure to them, in order that young people may grow into strong and confident adults.

Henson's images of youth show abandonment to frailty – something we are meant to prevent – and their nudity or near-nudity exposes them. Their nudity is not wrong in itself, but our viewing of it is. Moreover, children are innocent of the potentially evil motives of adults, and therefore unaware of the impact of their own naked images. The logic of sexual taboo means that adults are forbidden from looking upon a naked child, because such voyeurism taints the imagination and creates a desire to violate that the adult may not be able to control. The logic of safety is thereby inextricably tied to the logic of taboo. Also closely related to this is the assumption that desiring young people is morally reprehensible. Thus the widespread abhorrence and condemnation of what was seen as Letourneau's seduction of her student also reflects the logic of safety and the moral temporality of sexual taboo.

The temporality of body functionality

The way bodies are governed in western society tells us a lot about what is expected of individuals. Bodies function to normalize[23] and, moreover, bodies are normalized through the consumption of clothing and related products such as beauty services. Young people become aware of the impulse to normalize, and the disciplinary control required to achieve it, at a very young age. Adults love to dress up their children and school them in how to behave in public, and this is reinforced by peer pressure and representations of children in the media. Henson's youth, however, have no discipline. Several of the images show a naked young man or woman lying wantonly across the body of a car, or wandering aimlessly across a bleak landscape. These youth lack restraint both because they do not cover themselves, and also because they do not use their bodies in acceptable ways that mimic what is considered to be normal. Henson's images thereby challenge and overturn what is considered to be acceptable bodily presentation and performance for young people. And while there are certainly other artists and photographers who depict rebellious or disenfranchised youth, it is the combination of disenfranchisement and nudity that finally condemns Henson to the label of paedophile. Young people may be forgiven for transgressing some norms – they are, after all, not yet fully reasonable adults – but when those transgressions invite the performance of taboo activities, such as that which "necessarily" invites adults' desiring of them, then they – or their inventor–artist – must be disciplined and sanctioned.

The increasing functionality of bodies is aided by modern medicine and psychiatry, which seek to alter bodies to conform. Elizabeth Grosz argues that bodies are marked and coded through clothing, jewellery, make-up, cars, furniture and other consumer goods. In this way, the rest of us are able to read the codes and markers, and make judgments about normality and acceptability. She argues that these codes "bind individuals to systems of significance".[24] Children, in particular, are marked and coded in this way through school uniforms, classroom regimenting, and institutional and familial socialization, which ensure that significant systems are perpetuated and reinforced. Again, Henson's youth are threatening to these regimens because they have discarded their coded functions and therefore present as both a risk to normality and as bodies that now need to be protected.

Bodies are also gender-encoded from birth, either as male or female, and are socialized accordingly. Henson's images of youth often depict them as androgynous, and this challenges the gendered encoding of bodies, thereby further condemning him as deviant and dangerous. Judith Butler notes that gender is performative – that is, socially constructed both discursively, through language, and bodily, through physical performance. Thus, when a doctor utters the phrase, "it's a girl" or "it's a boy", he is discursively allocating gender to the infant, ascribing a female or male subjectivity that will determine its life-course.[25] That subjectivity encompasses an entire range of bodily performances learned throughout childhood and adolescence, and enacted in ways that clearly identify the person as female or male. Such performances are not a choice, but are constitutive of an individual's identity. In this sense, one just *is* one's gender identity.

In recent times, wealth, technology and improved education have meant that gender differences in terms of function and achievement have become blurred. However, children and young people are still expected to perform their gender according to hegemonic – that is, widely accepted and entrenched – masculinity and femininity.[26] The female child may be tolerated for her tomboyishness up to a certain age (which is usually puberty), when the expectations of feminine gender performance become more pronounced.[27] Young male children, however, are given less leeway. The male child who dresses up and paints his fingernails at age three or four may be the object of humour and tolerant acceptance by doting adults, but if he carries this behaviour on for too many years, he is ridiculed and ostracized as effeminate, "girly" or "gay", regardless of his actual sexuality.[28] The message children receive by the time they reach puberty is that gender performance is important – indeed, in some instances it means everything – and that deviating from the code has dire moral and social consequences.

Conclusion

The social construction of gender, sexuality and taboo is therefore temporally located in the discursive practices and bodily performances imposed upon individuals from birth and throughout life. The following two chapters take this observation as a starting point for exploring the construction of two highly controversial sex crimes. Chapter 3 investigates the temporal morality of incest, unpacking the notions of familial sex and the taboos surrounding it. Chapter 4 sets about deconstructing pornography in more detail, inviting us to examine the assumptions underlying our beliefs about the consumption of sexual media. Together, these chapters challenge our perceptions about the supposed universal and essential nature of the moral values underlying such sex crimes, encouraging us to take a fresh look at how our perceptions are shaped by the discourses of our time.

3

INCEST

Introduction

In April of 2008, in a small town in southern Austria, Josef Fritzl was charged with imprisoning his daughter for twenty-four years in a cellar in the family home, and fathering seven children by her. The crime shocked the world. Austrian police described the revelations as "one of Austria's all-time worst crimes". Guenther Platter, the country's Interior Minister, called it "unfathomable". The local newspaper called it "the worst crime of all time". Yet, despite its horror, police reported that Mr Fritzl, who they described as "domineering, aggressive and tyrannical", appeared unrepentant. What was so shocking about this crime, separating it from other, similar crimes, such as that committed against Natascha Kampusch, the Austrian teenager held captive in a Viennese cellar for eight years before escaping in 2006? The answer lies in both the extremity of the facts of the case, and the place incest currently occupies in our moral psyche.

According to news reports, Fritzl's daughter Elisabeth was eighteen years old when he drugged, kidnapped her, and locked her in the family cellar. The entrance to the cellar was hidden by a bookcase, separated from the world by a foot-thick door, with a security code known only by Fritzl. Over the years, he brought home letters from Elisabeth, dictated by him, which explained both her disappearance and the subsequent appearance of three babies left on the Fritzl doorstep and raised by Elisabeth's mother. The cellar that Elisabeth would call home for twenty-four years comprised sixty square metres, with no natural light and ceilings only five feet, four inches in height. Adding to the horror of the situation is a presumption that the four older children, who had remained in the cellar with their mother, had to watch their father deliver his daughter's subsequent children and be witness to the intercourse between father and daughter. While she claims that her father repeatedly raped her, he maintains that the sex was without force.

During the trial in March 2009, a psychiatrist told the court that Fritzl had a very serious personality disorder and would still pose a threat even at his advanced age.

Psychiatrist Adelheid Kastner recommended that Fritzl serve out his sentence in a psychiatric ward. Explanations for his crimes included the psychological damage done to him as a child by his "tyrannical mother" and the fact that Elisabeth herself was promiscuous and out of control on drugs, and that her imprisonment was to protect her from harm. Each of these explanations speaks to very recent understandings of familial sexual relations, the innocence of children and the predatory nature of men. In modern society, sex and taboo come together in the damage and danger of incest.

Prior to the late nineteenth century, incest was discussed only in relation to marriage and kin, most often evoked to challenge the legitimacy of a marriage between an uncle and a niece, or a husband and a sister-in-law. While this has little purchase on current understandings of incest as intra-familial sexual abuse, and demonstrates quite easily the temporality of moral authority, it would be wrong for modern audiences to assume that there was a lack of moral judgment about incest at this time. Indeed, there were very clear boundaries surrounding appropriate sexual relations, with affinal incest (that between married relations) treated with far more lenience by the community, if not the church, than consanguineous incest (that between blood relations). There were also acceptable lines of descent, where marriage between relatives was much more appropriate through paternal than maternal lines, and for the upper classes at least, a clear boundary across generations, such that marrying one's sister-in-law was sanctioned but marrying one's niece was not.

It is this recent moral boundary between generations, which proscribes sex with children as inappropriate, psychologically damaging and the result of a perverted adult desire, which has gained momentum over the past 100 years. Such an understanding, however, is also very recent in its construction, and relies upon certain ways of understanding children, not only as a distinct phase of life between infancy and adulthood, but also as innocent and lacking a sexual nature. Recall Aries's argument from chapter 2 that childhood was not identified as a separate phase of life until the fourteenth century and sexual innocence not attributed until the sixteenth and seventeenth centuries, culminating in the positioning of children as asexual in the nineteenth century. This understanding required a huge shift in sexual relations between children and adults, who had previously, irrespective of class, engaged in what would now be understood as "perverted ribaldry". However, by the end of the nineteenth century, all European nations had passed age-of-consent laws which demarcated sex with children under sixteen as not only bad for the child, but indicative of a lack of morality within the adult. Similarly, the criminalization of incest for the first time in the early twentieth century positioned familial sexual relations as morally inappropriate, especially among the urban working poor, where it was seen as both prevalent and inevitable. This understanding, promulgated by middle-class reformers, often misunderstood the clear moral codes that defined appropriate sexual relations for young people and within the extended family; however, it did speak to the tension within society regarding the boundaries of childhood, especially the idea that sexual experience and sexual knowledge is the *de facto* boundary separating childhood from adulthood.

Third, the differing ways in which sexuality in children has been conceptualized is linked closely to understandings of their body functionality, and this has had major implications for the ways in which incest is identified. Children in the sixteenth and seventeenth centuries were understood to have a sexual nature, and sexual relations between children and adults were considered to be nothing more than an acknowledgment of the child's innocent desire for sexual pleasure. In such a scenario, no "moral panic" over incest occurs. From the nineteenth century, this romantic notion of the child as uncorrupted by sexual relations with adults shifted to a more complex understanding, which acknowledged the sexual innocence of children while also identifying their potential for corruption. Children were both sexually endangered and sexually dangerous. At this time, incest became a major moral concern for society, but as problematic as the vice external to the child was the child's awakened sexual instinct. In the late twentieth century, a further shift in the understanding of relations between children and sex saw children as antithetical to sex, and any sexual relations with adults as implanting sexual knowledge in the otherwise sexually ignorant child. Now, incest is supplanted by child sexual abuse as the major threat to the moral fabric of our society.

Discovering incest

While incest has always been a crime against Christian morality, specifically condemned in the Old and New Testaments of the Bible, it did not become a criminal offence until the early twentieth century. This did not mean, however, that incest was sanctioned prior to this time. Rather, incest was dealt with through canon law in the ecclesiastical courts. However, the definition of incest upheld by these courts focused on marriage rather than blood relatives. Modern legal definitions of incest as intra-familial sexual crime do not fit easily with such an understanding, but they do offer an insight into the temporality of moral authority, in three ways.

First, the focus in ecclesiastical courts was the restriction of *marriage* rather than sex. In 1563, the Church of England adopted a *Table of Levitical Degrees* proposed by Archbishop Parker which enumerated the thirty blood and in-law relatives forbidden to a man to marry, and the sixty forbidden to a woman. Given that this Table was printed in *The Book of Common Prayer* of 1662, it hung in every parish church across the country. Importantly for our discussion, a prohibited marriage was "adjudged to be incestuous and unlawful".[1] The unlawful part was dealt with by Parker's *Table*, and such a marriage was retrospectively voidable, rendering all children of the union illegitimate; the incestuous part was separate and was subject to penalties of excommunication or public penance by the ecclesiastical courts. It is thus worth stressing that, in contrast to modern ways of understanding incest, relations of consanguinity (persons descended from a common ancestor) and affinity (created by marriage) were on precisely the same footing with regard to both forbidden marriage and incest.[2]

This is for a number of reasons. The most obvious is based on the English interpretation of the Old Testament, specifically the *Book of Leviticus*, chapters 18 and 20, which specified relatives who could not be married. Between 1215 and the mid-sixteenth century in England, these were up to and including third cousins by blood or in-law. Legislation enacted by Henry VIII between 1533 and 1540 permitted marriage between first cousins by blood and in-law, and only relatives closer than these were forbidden to marry.[3] This interpretation was based on notions of parity and argued that "consanguineous and affinal relatives being alike, any affinal relative was forbidden if the same consanguineous relative was expressly forbidden by Leviticus".[4]

This view of affinity is unique, and derived from the English conceptualization of marriage. As the heteronormative centrepiece of the English kinship system, marriage creates a relationship between the kin on each side such that a husband and wife take on each other's relationships. Each becomes the "in-law" relation of the other's blood relations, based on the idea that when two people married they became "as one". The integration of affinity with consanguinity can be seen in the strength of the opposition to affinal marriages in the early twentieth century.[5]

Second, the attention focused on incestuous marriage in the ecclesiastical courts was not transferred to sex outside marriage. Until 1857, when the *Matrimonial Causes Act* transferred jurisdiction over matrimonial causes to other courts, there was no distinction in the church courts between incestuous and non-incestuous intercourse outside marriage. All such sexual relations were punished as adultery. Their clandestine nature meant that illicit sexual relations often came to light only when an unmarried mother went to register her child before the clergy or magistracy.[6] The cases Morris[7] found of clergymen registering births as "incestuous" all involved stepfather–daughter incest, and "while the daughter may have been punished for bearing a bastard and the father may have been forced to provide support, they could not be punished for their incestuous sexual relation" because they were not married.

In this context, the "great majority of incestuous unions subjected to ecclesiastical scrutiny involved marriage between 'affines', or people previously related by marriage rather than blood".[8] However, given that such marriages often occurred after a spousal death and united two bereaved families, Morris suggests that "affinal sexual relations were not uniquely stigmatised".[9] In some cases it may have been a survival strategy, "determined by a widowed woman's economic dependence" or "a widower's need for a woman to run his house and raise his children".[10] Moreover, given that many "were solemnised in parish churches, it seems possible that they may have been tolerated or even encouraged by local authorities".[11]

Despite this less restrictive understanding of affinal incest, it was not until 1907 that the passing of the *Deceased Wife's Sister's Marriage Bill* legalized such marriages in England, though there was much opposition to the reform based on the belief that such toleration for affinal incest would lead directly to toleration for consanguineous incest.[12] Importantly for this discussion, the Act specifically declared that adultery between a man and his living wife's sister was to continue to rate as incestuous adultery, thus continuing the relation between incest and affinal relations. One year later, in 1908, the *Punishment of Incest Act* was passed, which criminalized incest for the first time in England. Affinal incest was not included in its definition, and the forbidden blood relatives were narrowed to those in the second degree. This meant that relatives forbidden to marry were, ironically, not committing incest, though amendments to the *Deceased Wife's Sister's Marriage Act* in 1921, 1931 and 1937 removed these final prohibitions.[13]

Third, with the focus of incest within marriage, those cases that come closest to modern understandings of incest as familial sexual crime were marriages that occurred between half siblings. They thus sat in the nether region between affinal and consanguineous incest. As Morris notes, "in a society where marriages were frequently broken by death and remarriage was not unusual, half siblings abounded … the death of their parents could create dependencies that were strengthened by differences in age and gender".[14] However, there were moral rules within such marriages which specified that those half siblings who shared a father were related within acceptable bounds, while those who shared a mother were not. This was irrespective of the age differences, which often spanned a generation. Thus paternal and maternal descent, like affinity and consanguinity, differentiated acceptable from non-acceptable incest within the community, if not the church. Interestingly, affinal marriages within the higher social classes most commonly sought a new partner from their own generation (sister or brother-in-law), while those of the plebeian classes were much more likely to look to the generation beneath them (nephew or step-daughter). Such choices by the plebeian classes, as Morris notes, "would have been particularly distasteful to members of the upper classes, whose ideas of incest were more closely related, in the nineteenth century, to feelings about the sanctity of the home and of affective relations within the nuclear family".[15] This more "contemporary" morality that connects incest with children and the heterosexual nuclear family points to a morality "out of time" between the two classes.

The modern expression of horror inspired by incest, reserved for sexual relations between blood relations, has a recent history. Certainly, biological arguments about the ill-effects on the progeny of consanguineous unions, which might be argued to be a dominant explanation for this ongoing abhorrence, were scarcely mentioned in the parliamentary debates leading to the *Punishment of Incest Act* in 1908. Moreover, the assimilation of affinity with consanguinity was made most clear when relations of affinity were included as amendments up to and including the passing of the 1908 Act. However, historically, sanctions against incest were always based on heterosexual alliances; there is no mention whatsoever of the possibility of incest between same-sex relations, whether affinal or consanguineous, probably because the notion of incest was tied so tightly to the concept of marriage and heterosexual kinship relations. While such historical understandings of incest have been lost to popular consciousness, they demonstrate both the moral and religious underpinnings of social and cultural concern over incest, and also that such prohibitions are modified by sexuality, class, culture and historical context. Such an understanding can also serve to destabilize the dominance of scientific explanations for an "incest taboo", focused on eugenics since the early twentieth century, especially since they ignore influential debates about the temporality of sexual development and the sexual innocence of children.

The rise of innocence

The enactment of legislation in the early twentieth century making incest a criminal offence has been argued to be part of a wider concern to articulate the sexual innocence of children and their need for protection through the domestic realm of the family, a concern that led to what Scott and Swain[16] term the child rescue movement. This way of thinking about children was promulgated by the rising middle class of the nineteenth century, and informed by what Weeks describes as "intensified emotional investment in the child and a fear of sexual corruption".[17]

The romantic notion of the innocent child lost ground from the mid-nineteenth century to a more scientific understanding of the child and childhood sexuality, which recognized a sexual instinct existing from birth, but positioned it as dormant, unconscious, latent. Children were innocent precisely because they had no sexual knowledge, yet at the same time children were perceived as at constant risk from external corrupting influences on their sexuality. The child became a sentimental figure in need of protection, and an object of suspicion that needed to be controlled. The most common causes of this external corruption were a "knowing" companion, a poor environment and bad parenting. A good home and appropriate parenting became crucial to safeguarding the sexual innocence of children.

Understanding children as especially vulnerable to external corruption culminated in a series of social surveys of the urban poor between the 1840s and 1880s in both England and Australia. The subsequent discovery of the widespread nature of single-room living for vast numbers of working-class families focused concern on the relationship between overcrowding and the enforced immorality of the poor.[18] This became, for middle-class reformers, a growing concern over incest. It is certainly true that the small size of dwellings in colonial America, for example, allowed working-class children quite early in their lives to hear or see sexual activity among adults. "Although curtains might isolate the parental bed, all family members commonly slept in the same room, especially during winters when a single fireplace provided the heat."[19] In Victorian England, this was compounded in working-class families by the common practice of sharing beds, and the fact that boys and girls tended to remain at home until they were adults.[20]

However, as Weeks suggests, "there is plentiful evidence that the working class had a very clear set of ethics of their own which survived for a considerable time".[21] "Bundling", which enabled intimate but fully clothed and ritualistic forms of petting, cuddling and courtship in bed, is one example of an earlier tradition that survived into the nineteenth century. It was also a common rural tradition right up into the nineteenth century that sexual relationships could begin at betrothal to a steady boyfriend. Such pre-marital sexual relationships were characterized by all manner of mutual masturbation and fondling, but very little actual penetration.[22] This enabled the couple to avoid the sins of fornication and adultery as well as pregnancy, with the latter a significant cue for marriage at this time. While these practices may have disappeared from middle-class homes by the beginning of the nineteenth century, they did not disappear from working-class families until the end of that century, and it was, in part, this difference in understanding of childhood as sexual innocence between the classes that enabled the *Punishment of Incest Act* to be passed in 1908.

By the nineteenth century, the separateness of childhood had clearly become entrenched in Victorian ideology, with greater emotional involvement in the welfare of the child and increased parental authority being encouraged within the family.[23] Central to this new relationship was the denial of certain types of behaviour between parent and child, with sexual contact specifically excluded.[24] It is within this historical context of the "child as innocent" that age-of-consent laws were passed through most parliaments in the western world.

The enactment of age-of-consent legislation defined, for the first time, appropriate intergenerational sexual relations both inside and outside the home. In England, the *Offences Against the Person Act* of 1861 established twelve years as the age of consent for young women, as a means of protecting them against the harm of sexual exploitation. Interestingly, boys were specifically excluded from this Act, even though they too might have been defined as children and open to the harm of exploitation under the age of twelve.[25] Further changes were made to increase the age of consent to sixteen through the *Criminal Law Amendment Act* of 1885. Colonial Australia followed a similar pattern, and in New South Wales, for example, the *Criminal Law Amendment Act* of 1883 raised the age of consent to fourteen, while the *Crimes (Girls' Protection) Act* was passed in 1910, further raising the age of consent to sixteen. However, this later Act specifically excluded girls of fourteen or fifteen from its protection if they "looked" over sixteen.[26] In South Australia, the *Criminal Law Consolidation Act* (1885) raised the age of consent to sixteen. In Victoria, the *Crimes Act* of 1891 raised the age of consent from twelve to sixteen. In Queensland and Western Australia in 1891 and 1892, respectively, the *Criminal Law Amendment Acts* raised the age of consent from twelve to fourteen. Tasmania raised the age of consent to eighteen in 1924 through the *Criminal Code Act*.[27]

Finch[28] argues that these laws emerged as the direct result of a desire to demarcate the social age barriers at which a person could be considered and treated as a child, as well as demarcating a line between the sexual and non-sexual person, with the non-sexual child being "out of bounds" as a sexual partner. In such a cultural and social context, all representations that acknowledge children's sexuality are subject to legal sanctions, as chapter 2 noted with regard to Bill Henson's art exhibition in Australia. However, such a demarcation also serves as a boundary separating childhood from adulthood, and thus creates a tension between the childhood victim of sex and the child who is "too knowing" sexually. The belief that sex under the age of sixteen is morally damaging, unnatural and psychologically harmful rests on a number of modern assumptions, not only about the sexual innocence of children, but also about the incapacity of the family to protect the child, based on a failure of the parent, normally the father, to have internalized this social taboo.[29] Such a clear demarcation also serves to deny any discussion of children's rights or needs as sexual beings in its assumption that sexually innocent (unknowing) children can only be traumatized by exposure to sex prior to the age of consent.

The problem of child abuse

As we have already seen, by the beginning of the twentieth century, a range of legislation, both criminal and social, instituted a way for society to patrol the borders between acceptable and unacceptable socialization of children, between acceptable and unacceptable behaviour among young people themselves, and between acceptable and unacceptable sexual practices. As Smart[30] notes, "we have a number of quite subtle boundaries being established ... Licit sex is not merely defined as that between married (i.e. heterosexual) couples, but between people of acceptable age brackets and doing only acceptable things." This shift in understanding of the relationship between children and sex is crucial to these boundary discussions.

The diary of Jean Héroard, physician to Henry IV of France, is an interesting case in point. Héroard's depiction of an extraordinary tolerance of children's sexuality, with a specific focus on a very young child's sexual behaviour, has been interpreted by some modern commentators as unacknowledged sexual abuse. Consider the following:

> When Louis XIII was not yet one year old: "He laughed uproarishly when his nanny waggled his cock with her fingers". An amusing trick which the child soon copied. "Calling a page, he shouted 'hey there' and pulled up his robe, showing him his cock."
>
> On another occasion, he was one year old: "In high spirits," notes Héroard, "he made everybody kiss his cock. This amused them all in the court."
>
> And finally, "The Marquise often put her hand under his coat; he got his nanny to lay him on her bed where she played with him, putting her hand under his coat," "The Queen, touching his cock, said 'Son I am holding your spout'."[31]

During his early life, the jovial and common act of touching the child's sexual parts was seen as a humorous interlude, with no harm, or intention of harm, involved. Here, children are expected to be interested in sexual matters. In this romantically inspired vision of the child, childhood, purity and innocence were linked in the social psyche. Sexual knowledge did not corrupt their innocence.

By the nineteenth century, however, this romantic notion of the child as sexually pure and incorruptible by adult sexuality had shifted to a more complex understanding of the child as both sexually innocent and yet open to corruption. From this time, children were seen as both passive and in need of protection, and yet also at the mercy of the "environmental contagion" of their sexual instinct. For example, girls raised by prostitutes could "catch" the deviance of their mothers, while a corrupt social order and over-abundance of "licentious" individuals in the city were particularly dangerous to children. Access to "immoral and prurient influences" promoted the appearance of the sexual instinct, at an age "much younger than nature ever designed".[32] Any expression of children's sexuality as "prematurely adult" positioned it, and the child, as an "abhorrent manifestation".[33]

Moreover, the home was so crucial to the protection of childhood innocence and the management of appropriate sexual behaviour that, if the construction of a suitable moral sphere was impossible, many reformers felt it better to remove a child altogether. Such concerns gave rise in part to the establishment of various Child Welfare Acts in the late nineteenth century, which enabled children to be removed from dangerous and/or inappropriate familial environments. In terms of inappropriate and/or precocious sexual behaviour, this was most often focused on young women, with institutions for wayward girls focused on restoring in them "the virtues of true womanhood".[34] However, such institutions maintained an ambivalent relationship with these sexually knowing young women, regarding their precocious sexuality as base and instinctual, and the result of weakness and a lack of inhibition and moral fibre.[35] In such a way of thinking about children and sex, the initiation of sexual consciousness too early was seen as dangerous for both other children, and society at large.

The sexually knowing child was a constant reminder of the work that needed to be done by parents and society to maintain childhood innocence, since the presence of any sexual subjectivity was evidence that damage had already taken place. The "knowing companion" was a particular target of moral reformers at this time, since a child with sexual knowledge was no longer innocent, and was a potential corruptor of other children. "Disreputable companions" promoted deviance by providing instruction on sexual vice in the school yard.[36] Sexually active children were also a threat to the moral fabric of society. They were perceived as a precocious menace that risked compromising the future of the entire society. The variety of programmes, policies and interventions that were instituted from the later nineteenth century by governments, churches, medical and psychological professions, as well as charity organizations, bear witness to this growing concern over the regulation of children's sexuality. Such knowing children, already adult in their sexual knowledge, removed themselves from the protection of childhood. They became actors in their sexual relations.

This explicit sexual discourse on children seemed to fade away during the 1960s, however, and the first formal acknowledgment of the problem and danger of sexual abuse within the family came with the passage of the *Child Abuse Prevention and Treatment Act* in the United States in the 1970s.[37] Positioning the child essentially as a victim of harm, this legislation marked a major break with earlier discourses that emphasized the sexual instinct. Children were perceived as "powerless", "unknowing", and "unable to consent"; there was "a presumed lack of sexual knowledge" and "an inability to make or understand sexual decisions".[38] This is a very different understanding of the relation between sexuality and children noted in the court of Henry IV of France, but it is also a different understanding of the relations between children and sex promulgated in the later nineteenth and early twentieth centuries. While the latter formulations placed great emphasis on a lack of sexual knowledge in children as a crucial part of their innocence, they also perceived children as having a sexual instinct, an inherent sexuality that was just below the surface and that could arise at any minute.

This more recent positioning of children as antithetical to sex has two important ramifications for our understanding of the relations between children and sex. First, child sexual abuse takes on the qualities of a universal diagnostic term, such that victims are not only irrevocably damaged, they are also forever outside normal sexual relations. The trauma of child sexual abuse follows the victim into adulthood, where "the failure to marry or promiscuity seems to be the only criterion generally accepted in the literature as conclusive that the victim has been harmed".[39] Second, although a focus on the asexual innocence of the child would seem to support the blameless status of children, the fact that sexual knowledge is also the boundary between childhood and adulthood marks out the victim of child sexual abuse as "too knowing". A child who "sexually responds to the abuse, or appears flirtatious and sexually aware" is judged against the romantic norm of childhood innocence. The "no longer virginal child becomes damaged goods" and "violating such a child becomes a lesser offence", with such children often seen as targeted for further abuse.[40]

Within this emotionally charged arena, there can be no discussion of children's rights or of their sexual needs, and no entertainment of the possibility that exposing the child to sexual activity might be a positive experience.[41] Yet, at the same time, the eventual move to engage in (hetero)sexual behaviour is normal, expected and a social achievement. In fact, in many parts of the world, the chief task of parenting is to prepare children for adulthood in terms of labour and reproduction.[42] In this current context, the rights of children as sexual beings can be understood only in terms of their right to protection from sexual exploitation. There is no way of thinking about the sexuality of children in terms of sexual agency. The outcome of such ways of thinking about the relationship between children and sex is to prolong childhood and to infantalize young men and women. Moreover, the disparities between the age of sexual consent (sixteen) and that of criminal liability (thirteen to fourteen) is particularly pointed.

The shift in the body functionality of children in the past 300 years has been from sexual knower, to sexual danger, to sexual innocent, and this has demonstrated a change in the ways in which the relationship between children and sex have been understood. In the court of Henry IV, the innocence of children was their protection from the corruption of sex. Children were assumed to be interested in sexual pleasure and to have sexual knowledge. In Victorian England, the innocence of children was a battle with the sexual instinct, which was always on the verge of erupting. Children were innocent until they had sexual knowledge, then they were a threat to be managed. In modern society, any relation between children and sex is a problem. Healthy children are asexual. Children with sexual knowledge are victims. Healthy asexual children are afforded the protection of the innocence of childhood. Children with sexual knowledge are damaged goods. There is no place in this new configuration for a discussion of the body functionality of children in sexual terms.

Conclusion

Sexual abuse of *some* children, which is actually usually constructed as sexual precocity of those children, illustrates the sexual innocence of *most* children. The sexual abuse by *some* fathers of their daughters illustrates that sexual relations in the modern family are *normally* very rigidly confined to the conjugal couple.[43]

This chapter has argued that morality and taboo come together in the modern psyche over a concern with incest, which is defined as "sexual contact, whether genital or not, between father, or father substitute, and child inside a single family unit". This conception is based upon recent ideas about the innocence and asexuality of children, the predatory nature of men, and the harm and damage of such abuse to the victim. These three elements were most evident in the case of Josef and Elisabeth Fritzl, and we hope our discussion here has gone some way to explaining why this case attracted such horror and outrage. Most likely, however, it was concern over the long-term effects of such a situation on Elisabeth and her children which speaks to this recent articulation of moral and social concern over incest: the ongoing damage to survivors and their inability to recover and lead normal adult lives.

The fact that older understandings of incest are now lost to popular consciousness demonstrates a temporality of morality which underpins this discussion. Religious concerns over marriage between affines seems far removed from the intra-familial abuse that dominates our understanding of incest today, but as the debates around the *Punishment of Incest Act* in 1908 demonstrate, such proscriptions were long-held and meaningful, and narrowing the definition to sexual relations between blood relatives was seen as a threat to social order. Interestingly, the *Punishment of Incest Act* narrowed the definition of incest so much that many relatives who were otherwise prohibited from marrying were not prohibited from engaging in sexual relations.

However, it was the creation of a distinct phase of childhood that has had the most impact on the way in which we have come to view the moral taboo of incest. Identifying children as distinct, innocent and asexual created a phase of life that not only was distinguishable from adulthood, but also was both dependent on and at risk from adults. Positioning children as sexually innocent required them to be protected from adult sexuality until they were developmentally capable of adult decision-making and responsibility – manifested in the legislating of the age of consent. However, positioning children as incapable of sexual consent was to position sex as the boundary between childhood and adulthood. This has had specific consequences for victims of sexual abuse in the later twentieth and early twenty-first centuries.

Such shifts in the moral understanding of the body functionality of children, from seducer to victim, had the largest impact on modern understandings of incest. In fact, its "discovery" in the 1970s, in the wake of a concerted feminist challenge to other sexual assaults such as rape, saw child sexual abuse, defined as incest of daughters by fathers, as *the* harm to which children were at risk. This was despite the fact that reports of child sexual abuse have never been higher than 8 per cent of all child abuse in either the USA or Australia. Moreover, a focus on the long-term damage to victims caused by child sex abuse saw such abuse become not only an explanation for all manner of sexual deviance, but also a way of policing the sexual behaviour of survivors: the sexually knowledgeable child is at greater risk of sexual exploitation.

Finally, such a way of thinking about incest rests upon an assumption not only that children are damaged by sexual relations, which interrupt the natural progression of sexual development, but also that any encouragement of sexuality in children is the result of deviant and perverse adults. This is despite research that shows that the most common type of sexual abuse against children is that inflicted by another child or adolescent.[44]

Incest has a long and varied history. Our modern understanding has enabled incest to be named, perpetrators to be punished and victims to be treated. However, this new incarnation of the moral taboo of incest is the culmination of 150 years of social and legal concerns over children and sex. Certainly, such acts are harmful and abhorrent in the context of the twenty-first century, but the belief that a large proportion of the population is at risk of such harm is misleading. Such a focus on the harm of sex for children under the age of sixteen also ignores the fact that, within the criminal justice system, children as young as thirteen years of age are held to be capable of reason and intent. This differentiation between criminal responsibility and sexual responsibility highlights both the arbitrary nature of the age of consent and the clear boundary between sexual knowledge and childhood.

4

PORNOGRAPHY

Introduction

Several years ago, a Supreme Court judge in New South Wales, Australia dismissed an appeal case regarding pornographic cartoon characters taken from the long-running family television programme *The Simpsons*. The case appealed against an earlier conviction for using a computer to access, and being in possession of, child pornography involving *Simpsons* characters. The appellant was found to have had sexually explicit cartoons involving Simpsons child characters Bart, Lisa and Maggie, remodelled with human genitalia and depicted in various sex acts. This was a landmark case, the core issue being whether it was possible for a fictional cartoon character to legally depict a person. The judge dismissed the appeal and upheld the conviction, even though it was noted that "the hands bear only four digits and the faces have eyes, a nose and mouth markedly and deliberately different to those of any possible human being".[1]

The dismissal of the appeal case and upholding of the conviction was widely questioned, sparking worldwide media coverage. A *Google* search at the time of writing reveals mention of the case in approximately 402,000 websites, including sites in the United States, the United Kingdom and Australia. Even lawyers challenged the judge's decision: "These sorts of parodies, offensive as they might be, are widely distributed and I think it would be very unfair to characterize those who are viewing the images as ... viewing child porn".[2] Of particular significance, then, is the argument made by the judge during the court process:

> Although the primary purpose of the legislation is to combat the direct sexual exploitation and abuse of children that occurs where offensive images of real children in various sexual or sexually suggestive situations are made, it also is calculated to deter production of other material – including cartoons – that ... can fuel demand for material that does involve the abuse of children.[3]

The judge's decision to uphold the ruling on the basis of protecting children and deterring offenders demonstrates very recent but, as we have seen in chapter 3, quite insidious assumptions about the inappropriateness of linking children, even cartoon children, with sex. Although the Simpsons characters are not real children, the ruling in this case suggests that sexually explicit representations of child cartoon characters are part of the moral taboo surrounding children and sex. It is also supported by the belief that viewing sexual activity, especially child sexual activity, is an act fraught with harm, a topic of much concern to psychologists,[4] who argue that pornography can be harmful to young people in particular.[5] Such concern is compounded by examples such as the now infamous serial sex murderer, Ted Bundy, who claimed that an addiction to pornography drove him to sexually assault and kill women.[6]

These concerns about pornography are inherently modern ones, related to the growth of pornography in the eighteenth century through the availability of print technology, and the subsequent development of visual as opposed to literate forms of sexually explicit material.[7] Indeed, it is only in recent times – from the nineteenth century – that pornography has come to be a target of suspicion and suppression, due in great part to the widening of its appeal to the illiterate, which included children. Despite constant and increasing attempts to regulate pornography in modern times, however, the commercial pornography industry goes from strength to strength. In the United States, for example, the pornography industry alone "has been conservatively estimated as worth something in the region of $10 billion per year, with an annual output of between 10,000 and 11,000 films, compared to Hollywood's 400".[8]

This chapter charts key discursive shifts that have led to modern ways of thinking about pornography as a morally contentious issue. By contextualizing the modern links between pornography and obscenity, we will chart the shift from a public discourse of sex, where sex formed a prominent part of much reading material, and was consumed as part of the public discussion of sexual matters, to the private consumption of pornography, which was created as sexually explicit material specifically designed to elicit a sexual response. Moreover, this shift from sex as a public discourse to sex as a private discourse was accompanied by larger shifts in the regulation of sexuality, especially for women and children.

This shift in the policing of women's sexuality, in particular, can be traced in part to a significant change in the way in which male and female sexuality was understood between the eighteenth and nineteenth centuries. Prior to the mid-nineteenth century, female genitalia were assumed to be the inverse of male genitalia. This meant that relations between orgasm and conception were assumed for both men and women. The subsequent discovery of the irrelevance of an orgasm severed the link between pleasure and sex for women, which had much to do with changing notions of femininity as passive and asexual.

Finally, current perceptions of sexual development, which, as we have seen in chapters 2 and 3, draw heavily on notions of sexual innocence and sexual purity, have been shaped historically by moral concerns about children and sex that came to the fore in concerns about masturbation, or solitary sex, linked specifically to the rise of visual pornography. The shift from literate to visual pornography is the moment when regulation is required to manage the working class and children, who, it was maintained, did not have the competencies to consume sexually explicit material.

Historicizing pornography

The word "pornography" was not to be found in the Oxford English Dictionary before 1864, and derives from the Greek word *pornographos,* which literally means "whore's story".[9] The distinctiveness of pornography, in comparison with the wealth of sexual material that existed prior to the nineteenth century, "was its explicitness and its intent to arouse a sexual response". While such material existed before this time, the mid-nineteenth century saw a major increase in the market and supply of pornography.[10] Moreover, while the control of these printed works in Europe between the 1500s and 1800s was undertaken primarily in the name of religion and politics,[11] by the mid-1800s it was the issue of decency that motivated regulation. In 1857, the *Obscene Publications Act* was passed in England, while in 1868 the *Hicklin test* entered English common law. These two changes have been identified as key to the identification of pornography as a specific social harm that threatened the moral health of the population.[12] Pornography, in the sense that we understand it today as a distinct category of written or visual representation, begins to exist significantly from the middle of the nineteenth century.[13]

It would be incorrect to assume, however, that sexually explicit material did not exist prior to its public and legislative regulation. According to Hitchcock,[14] the range of writings in which sex formed a prominent part prior to the nineteenth century was extensive. Such writing was to be found in publications aimed at both the educated elite (literature that was generally French in origin) and the plebeian classes (through joke books and "chapbooks"). Moreover, trial reports, accounts of divorce proceedings and medical literature were often read for their sexual elements. However, they were not yet pornographic. Rather, they were "always an adjunct to something else".[15] The widespread consumption of this material was reflective of a public culture of sex, "but it was more about the public discussion of sexual matters than they were aids to masturbation".[16]

Many historical accounts of sexually explicit material prior to the nineteenth century focused on sexual voyeurism as social, political and religious subversion. Hunt[17] notes how sexually explicit pamphlets were used during the French Revolution to undermine royal authority. Queen Marie Antoinette, for example, was targeted by pamphlets "detail[ing] her presumed sexual misdemeanors, question[ing] the paternity of her children and, in the process, fatally undermin[ing] the image of royal authority".[18] At this time, sexually explicit material was not an aim in itself, but rather an adjunct to other forms of criticism of church and state. Prior to the French Revolution, for example, prohibited books included those that threatened the state, religion or good morals. Moreover, they were all "indiscriminately labelled, 'philosophical books', whether they were politically motivated scandal sheets, metaphysical treatises, anticlerical satires or pornographic stories".[19] At this point in history, sexually explicit material may have been identified as problematic, but it was not a separate category of "bad books".

The employment of sexual behaviour in the service of social subversion was short-lived according to Wagner,[20] who suggests that these forms of sexual material faded into the background as new works were circulated that were "entirely devoted to sexual arousal".[21] The creation of sexual material designed only for the purpose of sexual arousal and as an aid to masturbation is the moment when modern pornography is identified as morally different from other "bad books", and the point at which sexually explicit material becomes the focus of policing and regulation for its implicit moral danger.[22]

It would be erroneous, therefore, to suggest that pornography has always been subject to moral and/or legal regulation, since modern conceptions of pornography as exciting "lascivious feelings"[23] were all but non-existent up until the eighteenth century. The excavation of Pompeii in the eighteenth century, and the discovery of sexually explicit artefacts in the homes, demonstrates clearly the shift that was occurring between older discourses that emphasized the harmless and public nature of sex, and newer discourses that positioned public displays of sex as physically harmful and morally inappropriate. For Kendrick, the archaeological excavation of Pompeii stands as the key historical moment where a shift is made evident in how people viewed sexually explicit material. As various sexual artefacts were unearthed, cataloguers of the eighteenth century struggled to classify these materials:

> Paintings of nude bodies, even in the act of sex, had been placed side by side with landscapes and still lifes, forming a jumble that mystified modern observers ... The problem was purely modern: however the Romans might have responded to such representations, what was one to do with them *now*?[24]

Modern classifiers were left somewhat bereft when faced with materials that existed in a time where "sex was clearly a common and unremarkable theme" – in Greek household items, for example.[25] In the eighteenth century, when sexual practices were increasingly relegated to private, domestic spaces, classifying these artefacts suggested the need for a new typology to ensure the proper management of "Pompeii's priceless obscenities". "Pornography" was the term employed for this purpose.[26] Even when precisely named, however, the classification of these materials was accompanied by much anxiety for those doing the work of classification:

> With this end in mind, we have done our best to regard each of the objects we have had to describe from an exclusively archaeological and scientific point of view. It has been our intention to remain calm and serious throughout. In the exercise of his holy office, the man of science must neither blush nor smile. We have looked upon our statues as an anatomist contemplates his cadavers.[27]

The classification work, then, became entangled with the work of managing "lascivious feelings", and contemporary sensibilities countered this by urging a moral imperative to regulate oneself in ways that lessened their sexual impact.

Although the classification of artefacts may have defined what was meant by pornography, this process, as Kendrick points out, "did not invent the obscene" and that which now is legally regulated.[28] Sexual texts have always existed, dominated by classical texts from Greece and Rome, and consumed as part of "a classical education [that] remained the privilege of gentlemen".[29] While such classical texts may well have inspired the reader to "lascivious feelings", the incitation of physical arousal as a result of viewing or reading sexually explicit material was purely incidental, not integral.

Consider the work of poet and artist Pietro Aretino (1492–1556), who created sonnets in 1524 to accompany drawings of sexual postures by Giulio Romano and etchings by Marc Antonio. By the nineteenth century, the name Aretino was synonymous with pornography. In fact, Aretino is hailed as "the originator of pornography" because his "licentious" work brought together "explicit sexual detail and evident intention to arouse that became, three hundred years later, the hallmark of the pornographic".[30] Aretino's work "combined precise sexual postures with explicit attitudes and feelings required to enact sexual activity in a variety of positions".[31] This work was erotic and obscene, but it was not yet pornographic. In the late sixteenth century, this immoral work was prohibited, but so were politically immoral works such as Machiavelli.[32] Moreover, classical erotic works were used in medical texts of the time, and there was no suggestion that these were morally inappropriate.[33]

The creation of a modern engagement with sexually explicit material also charts the creation of the category of erotic, lewd and obscene materials, which were identified for the first time as having a specific immorality within them, related to their function in sexual arousal. This new way of engaging and thinking about the erotic comes at the same time as an expanding print culture, which put the written and visual word into the hands of a large proportion of the population, as well as raising concerns over children and the working class and their involvement in sexual activity outside of middle-class norms of appropriate behaviour, as we have discussed in chapter 3. These concerns over sex, children and the working class required, among other things, controlling access to pornography.

Regulating pornography

Historians of the western world often document the impact of Judaeo-Christian ideologies on modern understandings of morality and sex.[34] It is well known that, prior to the introduction of Christianity, sexual activity – especially, but not only among the Greeks and Romans – was considered a site for pleasure and enjoyment, even beauty and truth. Plato's *Symposium*, for example, outlined a system for classifying sex and love in just those terms, almost canonizing the association of sexual love (between men at least) with conventional mores about the nature of social life. For the ancient Greek, pleasures of the body – including the viewing and enjoyment of naked bodies – were considered a right and an entitlement of citizens of the Athenian state. In contrast, early Christian texts positioned sexual activity for pleasure, rather than for the service of procreation, as ensuring humanity's fall from grace, given the relations between sex and "original sin" in the Garden of Eden.[35] For the first documented time in history, sexual desire and lascivious feelings become a moral issue. In fact, desire outside the confines of a procreative relationship signalled that the body "was possessed by evil forces, the presence of which were felt through the irresistible desires for sexual gratification".[36] Sex was in need of careful state and religious regulation, for if humanity was to amount to anything, people needed to deny their sexual yearnings in favour of pursuits such as hard labour, which was one of the vehicles, it was thought, for ensuring chastity and virginity were maintained. Ultimately, sex in Judaeo-Christian doctrine "was considered a dangerous force"[37] and sexual behaviour deviating from the procreative was subject to legislative and religious regulation.

This understanding of sex came to the fore in the nineteenth century, when, in America, for example, Anthony Comstock, whose famous anti-pornography campaigns caused pornography to be known as "Comstockery", "boast[ed] that his antismut campaign was responsible for the suicide of 16 producers or sellers of what he considered to be immoral materials".[38] In such a moral climate, any representations of sexual activity that sought to stimulate desire, or to encourage people to experiment with sexual variation, were subject to moral regulation and often criminalization. While people are no longer incarcerated for breaching these socially constituted boundaries of "good" sexual behaviour, the moral imperative to regulate pornographic materials for the sake of public protection continues to persist, most recently in the form of classification boards.

However, the regulation of pornography from the mid-nineteenth century was most often motivated by the potentialities of certain groups of people to be corrupted by pornography. This moral type-casting was generated particularly by upper-class, learned gentlemen who roundly condemned those deemed to be susceptible to the lure of pornography in its various forms. The most susceptible groups included women, children and the working classes, all of whom, it was claimed, "lacked intelligence". Women were of key concern as a group, because earlier pornography had typically taken the form of the novel, a technology that children and the working classes were assumed to lack the skills to access. Concerns about children and pornography were non-existent at the beginning of the nineteenth century, despite a thriving industry, because it was assumed that most children did not have the capacity to read and interpret these materials.[39]

Upper- and middle-class women, however, were another matter. From the late eighteenth century in particular, novel reading was a practice seen to be productive of a range of "physiological effects, especially in women because of their tender fibres".[40] Pornography, as a specialized version of the novel, "played upon the imagination of the reader to create the effect of real sexual activity". Women were thought to be especially susceptible to the "imaginative effects of the novel".[41]

Ultimately, the regulation of pornography was constituted in line with the assumption that there was a direct relation between consumption of sexually explicit material and moral harm, "for those that did not have the 'cultural competencies' to deal with this material".[42] The working classes in particular were seen as exemplars of this lack of cultural capability to process pornographic material in appropriate ways.[43] However, the exclusion of children and the working class from an increasingly large amount of sexually explicit material persisted until the late nineteenth century, when for the first time visual images of pornography started to outstrip written porn-ography.[44] More panic followed this technical innovation as, for the first time, children, "lower" classes, and other cultural and ethnic groups had access to obscene material. It was cheap and freely available, often being sold alongside newspapers and other forms of media, sparking concern by governing authorities. Where previously "vulnerable" groups had been informally excluded from such access, a process that was as simple as maintaining expense and illiteracy, visual pornographies rendered these forms of exclusion useless: "Postcards could be viewed at a single glance, rather than requiring time, the skills of literacy, the cultural referents of art and literature, or the languages of Greek, Latin, and French".[45] This shift spurred governing authorities to "crack down" on sexually explicit materials, a policy that was also endorsed in popular medical texts, with respected authors such as William Acton[46] making explicit links between the viewing of pornography and "abnormal" childhood in a section of his book *The Functions and Disorders of the Reproductive Organs* titled "Normal functions of childhood":

> In a state of health no sexual impression should ever affect a child's mind or body. All its vital energy should be employed in building up the growing frame, in storing up external impressions, and educating the brain to receive them. During a well-regulated childhood, and in the case of ordinary temperaments, there is no temptation to infringe this primary law of nature ... Thus it happens that with most healthy and well-brought up children, no sexual notion or feeling has ever entered their heads, even in the way of speculation. I believe that such children's curiosity is seldom excited on these subjects except where they have been purposely suggested.

The role of pornography in stimulating sexual arousal in children came to a head in concerns over the rise of masturbation.[47] While the relation between pornography and solitary sex was identified as a key concern for men in the late eighteenth and early nineteenth centuries, children were targeted as potential masturbators from the late nineteenth century, as visual pornography became more available.[48] For boys, in particular, the concern was that pornography would cause a precocious awakening of their sexuality which would drive them to seeking prostitutes.[49] Underpinning this concern about the corrupting potential of pornography for children was a contradictory understanding of the child as both innocent and dangerous – innocent 'victims' of pornography, they were also "constantly threatened by horrid temptations, open to stimulation and corruption, and in danger of becoming monsters of appetite".[50] The body of the child was invested with sexual significance in terms of danger and vice, and it was through the child's body that sexual purity and innocence could be assured.[51] Most importantly, even though it may well have been possible for a child to learn how to regulate their behaviour in ways that maintain sexual innocence, most regulation was externally imposed by governing authorities.

These concerns have persisted throughout the twentieth and into the twenty-first centuries. The regulation of television, for example, has been targeted for these forms of governance to ensure children are not adulterated by televised sexual content. Today, television is programmed and scheduled according to "codes of decorum designed to minimize the danger of causing offence",[52] and television content is now carefully scheduled, sanitized and expunged of sexually explicit material of any kind during the family viewing period.[53] This temporal regulation of television is the cornerstone of the viewing schedule, to the point that family-oriented programming dominates the period from early morning until the late-night watershed of nine or ten o'clock, depending on jurisdiction.

Pornography and solitary sex

While the nineteenth century saw an increasing moral panic surrounding middle-class women reading saucy novels, the use of pornography as a tool for masturbation was considered a greater danger for men. This understanding of the role of pornography coincided with an increasingly persistent discourse on the dangers and health risks involved with masturbation. As Laqueur[54] argues, although we cannot determine whether pornography inspired an increase in masturbatory behaviour, there is no doubt that "the spectacular rise of the genre in the context of the private reading of fiction certainly made the question of solitary sex far more exigent culturally than ever before". Masturbation was considered "the crack cocaine of sexuality; and it had no bounds in reality, because it was the creature of imagination".[55] Most importantly, masturbation had come to represent all that was morally and socially reprehensible, as well as being a sign of physical disorder and weakness.[56] As masturbation came to be inextricably linked to pornography, pornography came to be thought about as a serious social problem linked with disease, danger and moral vice. Most importantly, pornography was demonized as inciting people to indulge in private, prurient pleasures that distracted from the proper role of sex as procreational, rather than recreational.

A crucial element of this concern was that masturbation involved "spending" sperm,[57] the generative fluid of procreational sex: "semen was a vital fluid whose loss was intrinsically debilitating".[58] In *Onania, or the Heinous Sin of Self-Pollution, and All Its Frightful Consequences in Both Sexes, Considered*, a pseudo-psychological treatise on the dangers of masturbation, Tissot (1708, cited in Hitchcock, 2002)[59] mapped a "spermatic economy" within the male body. To spend semen was to relieve and deprive the body of vital generative fluids. *Onania* was so powerful a text in defining the dangers of masturbation that a new disease, spermatorrhea, was "discovered": "Defined as the excessive discharge of sperm caused by illicit or excessive sexual activity, especially masturbation, the disease was understood to cause anxiety, nervousness, lassitude, impotence, and, in its advanced stages, insanity and death".[60] The panic that emerged with *Onania* and the disease of spermatorrhea further entrenched into perceived wisdom the dangers of pornography in its capacity to incite and excite masturbation.

Interestingly, while women were specifically excluded from this debate in the nineteenth century, this had not always been the case. The notion of loss through ejaculation had once also applied to women. Shorter[61] argues that, from the second century, women were thought to ejaculate with orgasm and to contribute generative fluid in the process of conception. This corresponds with the Galenic model of male and female bodies being constituted respectively by heat and cold: women were characterized by cold and wet humours, while men were dominated by hot and dry humours.[62] Genitalia were thought to be the same in men and women, but men's greater overall heat was thought to drive the internal sexual organs "outwards to form the penis, scrotum and testicles".[63]

The belief that women could become men if the heat in their body increased through activities like masturbation was a common theme in medical texts of the time.[64] All people were believed to be on a gradient from male to female characteristics, depending on the amount of "humoral life essence" within each individual. It was argued that "autoerotic friction" produces heat and the potential for clitorises to become enlarged and penis-like: "excess heat in women indicates potential masculinity, and the inverted penis may expel itself and become visible if women become too hot".[65] Sex, while good for both men and women, "with a moderate sex life in marriage important to good health", was ironically more important to women's good health than to men's. Excessive loss of heat through sex for men could be debilitating, while for women the reverse was true, with "the green sickness, hysteria and a range of debilitating conditions cured by heterosexual sex or masturbation".[66]

It wasn't until the nineteenth century that medical practitioners documented for the first time the "anomaly" that women need not experience orgasm to procreate and conceive.[67] This gave rise to a new understanding of sex devoid of female orgasm, and discourses about sex at that time reorganized around the knowledge that male sperm was the "active" factor in the procreative process.[68] This understanding of procreative sex as not necessarily a vehicle for women's pleasure was ossified in Victorian understandings of femininity.[69]

Hitchcock argues that sex during this period became "increasingly phallocentric. Putting a penis into a vagina became the dominant sexual activity – all other forms of sex becoming literally foreplay".[70] This was vastly different from prior perceptions of sexual activity, which involved a variety sexual practices, most of which we now think of as foreplay. Sex rarely involved penetration, and when it did, it was essential for women to orgasm "as a sign that the ovum has been ejaculated from the ovary".[71] Once there was no need to focus on the sexual arousal of the woman to ensure procreative sex, the penis became the focus of heterosexual procreative sexual activity. The male orgasm became the most important part of the process and the female orgasm "became simply a feeling, albeit an enormously charged one, whose existence was a matter for empirical inquiry or armchair philosophizing".[72]

Such recent ideas about male and female body functionality appear to have shaped our contemporary understandings of pornography. One might argue, for example, that the constitution of much pornography is phallocentric, focusing as it often does on the erect penis and the "money shot". Moreover, the relationship between the erect penis and the classification of the pornography as "hard core" speaks to ongoing concerns about active male sexuality.

While for many, pornography is still considered to be the "final commercialisation and desecration of sex",[73] such opposition has continually lost ground to arguments that encourage liberalization, based on the notion that pornography is harmless, private and a companion to good sexual relations. Such a way of thinking about pornography since the 1970s has seen the introduction of a system of classifications and controls which have extended the rights of adults to use pornography. The point of such regulations are twofold:

> First, adults were regarded as entitled to read and view what they wished in private or in public; second, members of the community were entitled to protection (extending both to themselves and those in their care) from exposure to unsolicited material that they found offensive.[74]

At the same time, concerns about pornography in terms of the content categories of children, and of violence, are escalating. While a number of government inquiries in Australia have concluded that "there was no convincing criminological or psychological evidence that exposure to such material produced measurable harm to society",[75] they have specifically excluded child pornography and violent pornography from their conclusions. Commissions established in Canada and the United States specifically to investigate sexually violent pornography found inconclusive evidence on any direct relationship between viewing, attitudes and acting.[76] In terms of censorship, "explicit or gratuitous depictions of sexual violence against non-consenting persons" remains illegal in many countries, while material that includes "explicit depictions of sexual acts involving adults, but does not include any depiction suggesting coercion or non-consent of any kind" is rated as restricted (X) and is illegal in many jurisdictions.[77] Interestingly, "depictions of sexual violence only to the extent that they are discreet, not gratuitous and not exploitative" are rated R, which gives them wide circulation in society. The classification system is more focused on sex than on violence, and enables the most violent content in the least restricted sexual category. With regard to child pornography, there is no grey area – it remains illegal.

Conclusion

Although it has been argued that western popular culture has been "pornified"[78] – that is, pornography has been mainstreamed – it would be erroneous to assume this means that pornography has become socially acceptable. While explicit sexual images and texts may have filtered into more "mainstream" popular cultural forms, such as advertising, pornography still arouses suspicion as potentially dangerous and illicit, and still regularly raises the ire of political and religious conservatives. People's experiences with viewing and consuming sexually explicit materials are heavily censored through government classification and control. The individual is enrolled in appropriately self-regulating the line between what constitutes healthy consumption and the moral and psychological dangers of pornography addiction. Empirical research seeking to discover the harms of pornography is ever-burgeoning in the hope of finding a causal link that will finally justify the complete abolition of pornography from our culture.

The libidinal capacity of pornography is of central concern in its regulation in contemporary western culture. The capacity of texts and images to stimulate sexual desire links back to the adulteration of sexual innocence in children – and hence to the continuing regulation of pornography. The Simpsons case clearly demonstrates this link. Moral and criminal sanction of Simpsons pornography is linked to how we think about the body functionality of adults and the appropriate, healthy sexual development of children. Simpsons children ought not to have adult genitalia in the form of cartoon pornography, because such images are considered a danger to children – both from their own desires, and from the desires of the adults who look at those images. That those images are completely non-human and intended purely to amuse only emphasizes the arbitrariness surrounding our common-sense views about pornography, moral danger and sexual appropriateness.

Part 2

5

OUT OF PLACE

The moral geography of sex and deviance

Introduction

In an episode from the popular television series *Seinfeld*,[1] the main character – Jerry – enters a train carriage on his way to work one day and takes a seat near the door. After several stops, the train soon becomes crowded. It's early, and Jerry succumbs to the rhythmic shunting of the wheels on the tracks and the stuffy atmosphere, and falls asleep. When he awakens some time later, he is surprised to find that he is alone, except for another man sitting across from him, who is reading a newspaper. However, further investigation – it takes Jerry some time to wake up properly – reveals that the carriage isn't empty at all; rather, its occupants have crowded down either end of the carriage, leaving otherwise empty the space occupied by himself and the man with the newspaper. This in itself is surprising, given the sheer number of people present, but Jerry is even more surprised when he realizes that the reason for this strange evacuation of the centre of the carriage is that the man sitting opposite him has disrobed and is now completely naked.

This scenario points up the absurdity of the average person's response to public nudity. The man with the newspaper sits nonchalantly, disregarding the fear and offence expressed through the actions of the other commuters. Jerry is caught in a situation where he is exposed to something commonly regarded as wrong – even illegal – and must decide what to do. It is clear that the other passengers are disturbed by the man's nudity because they have distanced themselves from it as much as possible. The following exchange between Jerry and the man is instructive:

JERRY: Oooo-Kay. You realize, of course, you're naked?
NAKED MAN: Naked, dressed, I don't see any difference.
JERRY: You oughta' sit here. There's a difference.
NAKED MAN: You got something against the naked body?

JERRY: I got something against yours. How about a couple of deep knee bends, maybe a squat thrust?

NAKED MAN: Who's got time for squat thrusts?

JERRY: All right, how about skipping breakfast. I'm guessing you're not a "half-grapefruit and black coffee" guy.

NAKED MAN: I like a good breakfast.

JERRY: I understand, I like good breakfast[.] ... .

NAKED MAN: I'm not ashamed of my body.

JERRY: That's your problem, you should be.

NAKED MAN DROPS HALF OF HIS NEWSPAPER.

JERRY: Don't get up. Please, allow me.

This short exchange is interesting for several reasons. First, Jerry demonstrates a relatively socially "appropriate" response to the man's nakedness: "You realize, of course, you're naked?" The question is rhetorical because it is obvious to the viewer and to Jerry that the man knows he is naked. But the fact that Jerry makes a verbal observation about the man's nakedness – albeit sarcastic – indicates that he is both surprised and disturbed by the man's apparent disregard of social and legal niceties. So, why doesn't Jerry flee to the end of the carriage with the other passengers? The answer lies partly in the fact that this event occurs in the context of television comedy, where the different and the ridiculous evoke laughter as a way of countering discomfort. But we suggest that the other reason Jerry does not flee is that the writers of the episode seek to challenge viewers' instinctive reactions to public nudity. Jerry is surprised and possibly disturbed, but not alarmed at the man's nudity. Should he be? Jerry's response to the man's inquiry, "You got something against the naked body?" indicates he is more disturbed by the man's body size and aesthetic than he is by the fact of his nudity. The man's body apparently disgusts Jerry because he is overweight by common standards. Would Jerry have been completely undisturbed by the nudity if the man had been slim and/or muscled? If the naked person had been an aesthetically appealing woman? Clearly, the exchange challenges our instinctive discomfort about public nudity as well as sending up our entrenched attitudes concerning body size and shape. But why are such challenges regarded as comedic? In this section, we explore the concept of the public and what is considered to be acceptable in the public realm, with a view to challenging some of our common assumptions about, and attitudes towards, sexual deviance, illustrated through crimes of indecency and public offence. It also examines the differences between public and private space, how public space affects the criminalization of certain sex acts, and how the criminals associated with these acts are governed.

The concept of moral space

In this chapter, we aim to trace the historical development of the notion of space and unpack the rationale behind how spaces at large are governed, particularly with respect to sexual behaviour. We suggest that geographical space in our society is governed by heteronormative discourses and practices which are hostile to non-traditional sexualities and non-traditional sexual behaviour. In this context, public space is characterized as areas in which people do not have a choice about what they are exposed to – in other words, they are reliant on the discretion of others in determining what visible, tactile and audible experiences they will encounter. Because of the heteronormative nature of public morality, which privileges traditional institutions such as families and heterosexual marriage, public spaces are governed by legislation preventing individuals from engaging in acts considered as offensive to those ideals.[2] This chapter examines the nature and socio-historical development of those ideals, and challenges their claim to dominance.

As we saw from our example above, one of the most entrenched attitudes surrounding public space is the fear of public nudity. Public nudity generally is considered to be inappropriate or wrong, and in many cases is also illegal. People do not expect to see naked bodies in public space and are affronted when exposed to them without warning. Nudity is acceptable under certain circumstances, in certain spaces (mostly private) and with prior notice. The notion of public nudity is therefore linked to the notion of consent, a concept examined in more detail in Part 3. In contrast, this section focuses on geographies of sex, which appear to be dyadically delineated into public and private. This dualism also extends to sexuality – public spaces must, for the most part, be heterosexual spaces. There are very limited public spaces for non-traditional sexualities, and those that exist are hidden, or, if occupying visible public space, tend to be subcultural, rendered non-threatening by heteronormative laws and conventions. For example, the practice of "cottaging" – where sex between men occurs in public lavatories and similar spaces – is commonly frowned upon, and known "beats" are usually patrolled by police. Similarly, non-heterosexual displays of love and affection, even where participants are fully clothed, often are considered offensive and policed under "public obscenity" or "public nuisance" laws.[3] Heterosexual partners who engage in such public displays are more often tolerated, depending on the extent of the display. However, irrespective of the sexual preference, public sex is illegal and members of the general public are affronted when faced with such displays. This policing of sex and nudity in public spaces is far-reaching across cultures and ethnic boundaries, and doubly discriminates against non-heterosexuals, but the concept of space as a context for regulating sex is itself relatively new.

In the late eighteenth and early nineteenth centuries, space for the first time was seen by cartographers and geographers as something to be investigated, mapped and classified. Space was an "objective physical surface with specific fixed characteristics upon which social identities and categories were mapped out".[4] Subsequently, scientists began to see space as more complex – as a social experience with interwoven layers of social meaning. Marxism and radical approaches to geography also "began to see space as the product of social forces, observing that different societies use and organise space in different ways and to explain the processes through which social differences become spatial patterns of inequalities".[5] More recently, Doreen Massey[6] has defined space as:

> the product of the intricacies and the complexities, the interlockings and
> non-interlockings, of relations of the unimaginably cosmic to the intimately

tiny. And precisely because it is the product of relations, relations which are active practices, material and embedded, practices which have to be carried out, space is always in a process of becoming. It is always being made.

Sexual geography, therefore, is a dynamic web of relationships circumscribing how people interact with sexual practices and displays, whether in public or private, and how such sexual practices are governed. Significantly, sexual practice is not neutral, but is embodied in heteronormative interpretations of gender and sexuality, as well as the proper constitution of a relationship and what that stands for. This is most obvious in how children's sexuality is governed in terms of spaces.

Recent ethnographic research has found, for example, that parents, in relaying messages about sexual threats while also trying to maintain children's innocence, give out the erroneous message that public space is dangerous, while private space is safe.[7] Where children were able to roam the streets and play freely with each other in times past, they are now more often locked behind closed doors, and both play and school time is closely regulated to ensure they are protected from anything sexual – including, but not limited to, naked bodies, sexual intercourse, and the display of erotic images and scenes. This moral governance of the risk of sex for children in large part determines where and when nudity and sexual practices may occur. Think back to our discussion of classification boards and television viewing codes in chapter 4. Such moral governance also determines the timeframe for sex – sex has become associated with the night, and so where public spaces are allocated to "adult entertainment", they are temporally confined to darkness. Needham comments that daylight is always associated with and reserved for families, because children in particular have access to the realm of the public during the day.[8] Thus anything to do with sex or non-heteronormative values and ideals must be hidden away from them, and only brought out when it is safe to do so. Hence we find television content regulated so that shows offering content over and above a PG rating must be held back until the relevant watershed time – usually 8.30 or 9pm, when all children are safely tucked into bed. Similarly, adult entertainment must be confined not only to spaces where families are unlikely to congregate, but also temporally to the night time, following the television watershed or even later. This ensures not only that the unsavoury activities conducted in these venues will occur outside family time, but also that they are covered by darkness, rendering them less visible and thereby less threatening to wholesome heteronormative values.

Foucault comments on the regulation of public spaces in his work on madness and prisons. Prisons discipline populations within confined spaces through an interweaving of medical, policed, urban and national spaces.[9] This facilitates the "careful organisation of time, space, bodies and action"[10] and "condones particular associations but not others between different classes of people, specific forms of sexual encounter, and certain spaces and times for the 'doing' of the sex acts in question".[11] Similarly, Philo argues that there is a "collision of population, sex and space – an interest in the spaces of sex acts, sex work, sex workers, sexual diseases, sexual health and sexual policies" that governs the way in which sex is enacted in society.[12] While some theorists advocate ridding society of regulatory practices concerning sex, Philo acknowledges the doubtful success of such a move:

> Many would doubtless feel uncomfortable with such an outcome, wherein sex escapes its regulatory framing, and where the spaces that matter become those of the chance encounter, embodied performance and the very immediacy of bodily shape, form, reach and position.[13]

The way in which sex is regulated, then, speaks to a fear of embodied sex in real life and real situations, which in turn creates an artificial moral category of sexual deviance focused on indecency and offence.

The geography of decency

In our society, prohibitions abound against activities such as nude sunbathing, flashing, streaking, solitary or mutual masturbation, fellatio, and vaginal and anal intercourse in public.[14] Specific criminal charges against offenders include "indecent exposure", "public indecency" and "lewd conduct". The concept of moral decency stems from deeply entrenched heteronormative ideals such as family, monogamy and marriage, and implies, as Johnson states, that "impersonal, casual and anonymous sexual encounters have negative connotations ... as they stand in contrast to ideals of romantic love, monogamous relationships, and long term commitments".[15] Discussions of nudity and sexuality are loaded with moral subtexts that speak to public judgments about what constitutes a moral space and how that space is governed.

Regulation of prostitution and adult entertainment in public spaces is a case in point. Strip clubs and brothels must be kept apart from areas where families and children congregate. Bernstein notes that urban renewal often relegates these venues, which originally tended to spring up in inner-city areas where adults congregate at night to seek entertainment, to marginal areas so that families will be encouraged and welcomed to frequent these previously morally inappropriate public spaces.[16] The same situation occurs with beats, which are strongly policed to the point where public toilets may be dismantled or moved to areas that provide more surveillance. The moral geography of sex precludes the pairing of sex with families in public spaces. Public toilets are for use by families and are not to be used as sexual spaces, regardless of how surreptitious or discreet the encounter. This causes a problem for non-heterosexuals, who may by necessity be forced out of private spaces in order to find sexual experiences. Sex is a private relation, and where it is offered publicly, it must be hidden or separated. Thus men cannot have sex together in public toilets and prostitutes cannot solicit in public spaces, because both represent a threat to the heteronormative construction of urban/suburban life.

Panoptic devices such as closed-circuit television, patrols, lighting and architecture are used to maintain surveillance of public spaces deemed at risk for illicit activity – either sexual, or criminal, or both. Legg notes that "these geographies can include the organisation of the home, the comportment and performance of a walker in the street, the sexual spaces of a community, the drilling of subterranean water channels, [and] citywide administration",[17] to name just a few. Public spaces are thereby arranged in such a way as to confine risky areas to fully regulated spaces subject to ongoing surveillance and control.

An interesting outcome of all this geographical surveillance and renewal is that cities now are creating what Bell and Binnie have termed "commodified gay spaces".[18] Spaces are set apart for gay clubs and they become publicly identified as gay spaces. Gay clubs and other spaces occupy their own territory, but such spaces are still policed to ensure that activity is restricted to congregating and does not extend to sexual activity.[19] Indeed, it is just because gays and lesbians (and intersexed and transgendered individuals, etc.) are identified by their sexuality that they become a "danger" in need of regulating. The essentialized association of "gay" with "sex" means that gay spaces are *necessarily* viewed as sexual spaces, regardless of whether actual sex is occurring in them. This leads to the view that such spaces must be monitored closely to ensure they do not impinge upon wholesome heteronormative individuals without their consent. Moreover, although public discourses about sexuality are becoming more and more tolerant, and even accepting, they continue to serve to confine non-heterosexualities, a phenomenon discussed in some detail in chapter 7.

Sex and moral distance

Returning to our example of the naked man on the train, we can see how moral decency requires that individuals put distance between themselves and the indecent. Further examination of the exchange between Jerry and the naked man reveals some interesting observations about how people deal with indecency in public spaces. As the scene continues, Jerry picks up the man's newspaper and the scene cuts away to one of the other characters. Several scenes later, the other passengers are still jammed at either end of the carriage, but Jerry and the naked man are nonchalantly discussing baseball.

NAKED MAN: They still have no pitching. Goodin's a question mark. ... You don't recover from those rotator cuffs so fast.
JERRY: I'm not worried about their best pitching. They got pitching. ... They got no hitting.
NAKED MAN: No hitting? They got hitting! Bonilla, Murray. ... They got no defence.
JERRY: Defence? Please. ... They need speed.
NAKED MAN: Speed? They got Coleman. ... They need a bullpen.
JERRY: Franco's no good. ... They got no team leaders.
NAKED MAN: They got Franco! ... What they need is a front office.
JERRY: But you gotta like their chances.
NAKED MAN: I LUV their chances.
JERRY: Tell you what. If they win the pennant, I'll sit naked with you at the World Series.
NAKED MAN: It's a deal!

By this stage, Jerry and the naked man seem to be completely disregarding the latter's state of undress and are carrying on the kind of normal conversation any two fairly well-socialized heterosexual men might have. They engage in a kind of camaraderie during this part of the exchange, and Jerry even jokes about being naked himself. Meanwhile, the other commuters are regarding this strange pair with some fear. The physical distance between the other commuters and these two speaks to the importance of space in two ways. First, individuals in our society feel threatened by public nudity in direct relation to how close they are to it. Second, a train carriage is a public space, and failure to observe the rules of public space require immediate withdrawal from that space. Given that the passengers are a captive audience, they have no option but to put as much distance as possible between themselves and the perceived threat.

In his influential work on offence and harm, Feinberg[20] examines some hypothetical situations in which behaviour such as public nudity may be regarded as offensive. The scenario for Feinberg's discussion is a crowded bus, on which we, the readers, are invited to imagine ourselves sitting. He asks if there are "any human experiences that are harmless in themselves yet so unpleasant that we can rightly demand legal protection from them, even at the cost of other persons' liberties".[21] In particular, Feinberg is interested in sexual acts performed in public and why such acts, which are acceptable in private, suddenly become offensive when performed in public.[22] He notes that "[o]ur culture, of course, is far more uptight about sexual pleasures than about 'harmless' pleasures of any other kind".[23] How would we feel, he asks, if the seat opposite us on the bus were occupied by a young couple who were engaged in kissing? It might make us feel slightly uncomfortable, but we would probably dismiss it as youthful ardour, and discreetly look away, perhaps occupying ourselves with reading or looking out the window. But what if the couple were of the same sex? What if they were fondling each other under their clothes as well? What if the couple proceeded to have oral sex or sexual intercourse on the seat across from us? Our reaction would most likely be similar to the reaction of the other passengers on Jerry's train – our disgust would warrant that we remove ourselves as quickly as possible.

Feinberg speculates that this discomfort about sex in public derives "from the danger in, and harmful consequences of, sexual behaviour in the past – disease, personal exploitation, unwanted pregnancy, etc. – and the intricate association of sexual taboos with rules of property transfer, legitimacy, marriage, and the like".[24] Public nudity and public sexual behaviour are, he concludes, complicated psychological phenomena leading to vicarious embarrassment and public shame.

> [N]ude bodies and copulating couples … have the power of pre-empting the attention and absorbing the reluctant viewer, whatever his preferences in the matter. The presence of such things in one's field of perception commands one's notice … Moreover, the problem of coping, for many persons as least, is a bit of a difficult one, not insurmountable, but something of an unpleasant strain.[25]

Why is this the case? Feinberg argues that nudity and sex acts draw us to thoughts that are normally repressed, eliciting unresolved conflict between instinctual desires and cultural taboos. There is a temptation to see, to savour, to become sexually stimulated, which triggers the "familiar mechanism of inhibition and punishment in the form of feelings of shame".[26] He argues that acts such as homosexual sex and bestiality are "immediately and powerfully threatening. ... [L]ower-level sensibilities are shocked so that a spontaneous disgust arises. Male homosexual acts violate powerful taboos in our culture; they also threaten the 'ego ideals' of heterosexual men."[27] And yet homosexual acts and acts of bestiality that occur in private pose no threat whatsoever, though some individuals may continue to believe such acts are morally wrong. The idea that offence occurs only when such acts are witnessed in public speaks to the heteronormative allocation of public space to the family and all its associated paraphernalia.

The scenario of our naked man on the train, however, takes an interesting turn that seems to question the validity of this widespread attitude. Several scenes later, the naked man has put on his clothes again, and he and Jerry are getting off the train together, still deep in conversation.

NAKED MAN: I haven't had a hotdog at Nathan's for 20 years.
JERRY: First we ride the cyclone.
NAKED MAN: Chilly out.
JERRY TAKES A DEEP BREATH.
JERRY: Aah, French fries.

The two men then head off to the Coney Island funfair together. Clearly, the man's nudity has become passé and a friendship of sorts has formed out of their brief exchange. It might even be suggested that the man's nudity, and Jerry's eventual disregarding of it, has created some kind of bond between the two men. The message here is that people may be different, have different views about things such as nudity, but these may be overlooked or disregarded when the people in question share other interests. In the end, then, the writers of this episode are quite radically challenging viewers to question their beliefs about, and attitudes towards, public nudity and the people who engage in it. The fact that public nudity is incongruous and threatening makes the episode humorous, and yet we are left with the distinctly uncomfortable feeling that we would probably act in the same way as those passengers who fled to the back of the train.

The nexus of time and space

Discourses abound on the risk of public spaces, evidenced by the proliferation of institutions for managing the daily lives of children and those who interact with them. As we saw in Part 1, discourses on childhood have changed considerably over time, and the notion of childhood itself is therefore a social construction. Valentine[28] describes two contrasting narratives about the way we think about children. On the one hand, children are wild, possessed of primal instincts, and the road to adulthood is paved by learning to overcome or harness these instincts for social good. On the other hand, however, is the view – originally proposed at the end of the seventeenth century by the Cambridge Platonists – that children are born with innate goodness and have the potential to be corrupted by an evil world.

The eighteenth century saw these two views hotly debated,[29] with the second eventually becoming dominant.[30] This, as we have seen in Part 1, led to child labour reform, among other things. By the nineteenth century, education was seen as a way of instilling discipline – schools became "moral hospitals" – at the same time as the notion of the juvenile delinquent developed. The twentieth century then paved the way for the domination of family and the role of the mother in nurturing children. "Mothers in the UK are expected to be guardians of liberal-democracy by bringing their children up to be self-regulating."[31]

This view was reinforced in the late twentieth century through public discourses on "stranger danger" and other risks, exacerbated by the invention in the 1950s of the "teenager",[32] a category of social, emotional, sexual and physical development that further extended childhood into the second decade of life. During this time, and continuing on into the late twentieth and early twenty-first centuries, parental fears for children developed from a belief that children's safety in public spaces has deteriorated since their own youth. And yet the statistics indicate that the number of children killed each year by strangers in the UK hasn't changed over the past thirty years, "despite the fact that the numbers of people charged or cautioned for child pornography offences has risen by 1500 per cent since 1988, largely due to the increase in material available on the internet".[33] A similar picture has been found in North American research.

Parental fears about children and public space are therefore largely misguided. As Valentine notes, "children are more at risk in private space" and "from people they know ... yet parental fears imagine a geography of danger from strangers in public space".[34] The social construction of childhood as a period of innocence and vulnerability has led to the strongly held and widespread belief that children are more at risk in public spaces than adults, and that those risks are "inherently more serious".[35] Negotiating parenthood and raising children have thus become focused on managing risk. This attitude is encouraged by the media, who delight in reporting failures in the moral regulation of sex and children.[36] Katz[37] labels this media coverage as "terror talk" and claims that such "terrorizing contentions concerning violence against children in the public arena – from abductions and molestations to armed assaults and murders – weigh heavily on the public imagination".

City spaces are also seen as much more dangerous than rural spaces.[38] The concentration of populations in cities is seen to exacerbate the risks to children, not least through the allocation of public city spaces to erotica, adult entertainment and sexual commerce, all of which are much less visible in rural areas, which tend to be more family-oriented. The privatization of children's play and the "decline in children's independent use of space" have become *de rigueur* as media reports of child sexual abuse and child pornography continue to increase.[39] This constant surveillance of children and teens means they have very little privacy. The tendency of parents to create domestic tensions around home rules and to allocate different rooms to different purposes creates order along strong domestic boundaries. Teens, however, like disorder and weak boundaries,[40] and tend to rebel against the regulation of private spaces.

School, too, is a highly regulated public space, which teens experience as an acute lack of freedom. There is little in the way of public amenities for teens in both Australia and the UK,[41] with teens tending to be governed through sport and other extra-curricular activities, all of which attempt to occupy the teen's time and space in such a way as to dissipate risk. The teenager who chooses not to engage in such pursuits is frowned upon and regarded as "at risk" – either of "dropping out" or of becoming delinquent, both of which are seen as an *entrée* to a lifetime of moral risk and debauchery. Again, the media exacerbate this trend by creating moral panics around examples of "at-risk" behaviour, often exaggerating the causes and effects of such behaviours and events and placing them strategically within certain feared spaces such as "the street".[42] The moral geography of the street positions young people who frequent them as "out of place" – the acceptable geography of a teenage existence is delimited by heteronormative institutions such as school, sport, clubs, church and family. To step outside this bounded existence is to threaten the very fabric of the heteronormative imperative.

Virtual space, or cyberspace, is even more challenging to that imperative, creating as it does a new kind of public space, one that presents new risks and panics, especially regarding children.[43] Cyberspace has challenged the accepted view of public space, making it globalized and therefore extremely difficult to legislate. Identities may be hidden, adopted, or obliterated in the space of seconds or minutes, leading practices such as sexual commerce and adult entertainment to take on a whole new meaning. The fact that people may engage with cyberspace within the privacy of their own homes, and are able to disguise their identities, makes cyberspace a dangerous place.[44]

Actual space also overlaps with cyberspace to create even more risk for the vulnerable and innocent. Hayes and Ball[45] note that young and old alike use cyberspace to explore sex and sexuality. Indeed, the exploration of sexuality in virtual space is much easier than in "real life" thanks to the creation of virtual identities and the suppression of real identities, which allows individuals to access sexually explicit material, both educational and pornographic, without fear of detection. This virtual anonymity also may encourage young people to try out sexualities and sexual practices they would otherwise not have access to, and this fact has created another moral panic, this time surrounding children and cybersex.[46] Child pornography is more easily distributed in cyberspace, which by association becomes a sinister public space which authorities are anxious to control and monitor. Cyberspace is an especially dangerous place for children and teens, and therefore must be governed in order to preserve childhood innocence. Cyberspace is highly threatening because it encompasses everything that constitutes a public space and yet is all but non-legislatable. The internet escapes the net of moral geography because it avoids the usual panoptic regulation imposed upon public spaces by heteronormative institutions of governance. It is, in other words, a space of resistance *par excellence* to heteronormative values and ideals. For young people, this is a double-edged sword, because the trade-off they make in exchange for cyber-freedom and the self-managing of identity is exposing themselves to genuine danger, even if the likelihood of being victimized is relatively low.

Conclusion

The burgeoning of virtual space over the past few decades has challenged accepted notions about the duality of the public and the private. Where physical public space has been sanitized so that it is acceptable to families, it has created a series of sexual subcultures that are identifiable and governable outside that heteronormative public space. However, the virtually ungovernable character of cyberspace has allowed the divide between the public and private to all but disappear, at least in terms of the internet. This ungovernability of virtual space has created a veritable moral panic that has led to further and more strenuous efforts at governing, leading to a burgeoning of policies and legislation regulating sex and children's exposure to it. The fact that such policies and legislation do not work has not forestalled such efforts.

In chapter 6, we examine how the effects of the panic about sex and children spill over into the governing of private lives through the regulation of sex offenders. In that chapter, we explore the vigilante nature of the public response to sex offenders and challenge some long-standing assumptions underlying the treatment of these criminals. Chapter 7 interrogates how deviant sexualities are positioned in the public realm, and identifies several inherent contradictions in the way we think about sexuality and non-heterosexual practices and identities. In this way, we hope to destabilize current acceptance of the duality of the public and private, and the way those spaces and associated crimes are regulated.

6

SEX OFFENDING

Introduction

On 26 June 2006, an eight-year-old girl by the name of Sofia Rodriguez-Urrutia Shu visited a public toilet in a Canning Vale shopping centre in Perth, Western Australia, and failed to return to her guardian. She was abducted by a twenty-two-year-old male, Dante Wyndham Arthurs, who strangled her, removed her clothing, digitally penetrated her, and propped her naked body against the cubicle wall. Police collected evidence in Arthurs's home suggesting he had meticulously planned the attack, including "a bag in a wardrobe containing latex gloves, handcuffs and rope along with a collection of pictures of young girls and their addresses".[1] Arthurs pleaded guilty to wilful murder, deprivation of liberty and sexual penetration, and was sentenced to life in prison with a non-parole period of thirteen years. The non-parole period was recently revoked by the Western Australian Attorney-General Christian Porter, and Arthurs's case has been marked "never to be released", one of only three cases in Western Australia.

This case received extensive coverage in the national and international media and sparked overwhelming public outrage. This was further fuelled by allegations that Arthurs had previously been accused of indecently dealing with children, and that it was only because of flaws in the nature of police questioning that this prior case was dismissed. In the murder case, however, Chief Justice Wayne Martin ruled a trial by judge alone was necessary due to the pre-trial case publicity being categorized as "extensive, continuous and in some respects extraordinary".[2] Part of this publicity included the publication by a Perth radio programme of details of Arthurs's address, which resulted in a vigilante attack on his house. He was also the subject of extensive online vitriolic commentary, including calls for the death penalty. The family of the young female victim called for a public register of sex offenders in Australia. Interestingly, such a register would not have prevented a crime like this from occurring, as

Arthurs had not previously been convicted of a sex offence. Nonetheless, in the wake of this horrific crime, the public continued to insist upon the implementation of a sex offender register, and this response is typical in relation to similar crimes. The perception of danger in this case created a fear for the public safety of all children, which was regarded as seriously undermined.

In a world in which children are regarded as highly vulnerable, this incident became the paradigm of every parent's worst fear. However, this level of fear, of both sex offenders and public space, is a recent phenomenon, most evident in public discourse since the 1990s.[3] In fact, the significant shift from the 1970s, when sex offenders were perceived as pathetic men in raincoats, to the mass hysteria in the twenty-first century, where sex offenders are perceived of as manipulative, dangerous and predatory, is "a remarkable one".[4] Within this public discourse of fear, those who offend against children are subject to the most extreme hostility, "considered too abominable to even associate with murderers and other criminals".[5]

In such a context, this chapter addresses the ways in which we think about sex offenders as morally dangerous people requiring especial regulation in public space, and the two central influences on which this way of thinking is founded. The first is a traditional religious understanding of sexual immorality as a desire inherent in all of us, contrasted with, and yet related to, the nineteenth-century rise of medical understandings of dangerousness and immutability. More specifically, the emergence of the psychiatric category of "sexual psychopath" amalgamated religious assumptions about a lack of moral worth with medical assessments of dangerous predators. Insisting that sex offenders lack moral worth and are inherently dangerous appeased religious communities by demanding government protection of the private spaces of the nuclear family and the sanctity of marriage, while also satisfying the psychological need for controlling these offenders in public spaces. The latter part of this chapter reflects on how heavily we now restrict the movements, lives and residency of sex offenders because of their presumed inherently perverted and predatory, immoral and immutable characters, even though research suggests these forms of management are not very successful. Finally, the chapter challenges the taken-for-granted notion that sex offenders should be subject to ever-increasing punitive controls implemented to surveil their movements in public, often to the neglect of private spaces.

Public and private sex

The argument that sexual perversion as we currently know and understand it has always existed is based on Judaeo-Christian discourses linking sexual sinfulness and humanity's fall from grace.[6] Here it is argued that feelings of desire were increasingly regarded as problematic from the fifteenth century because the body "was possessed by evil forces, the presence of which was felt through the irresistible desires for sexual gratification".[7] From this perspective, sex was rigorously controlled and only permitted in the form of "Godly" procreative, vaginal sex between a monogamously married man and wife: "Sex, except within marriage and then normally in the missionary position, was undesirable (at best) and illegal (at worst)."[8] Sexual acts other than those supporting procreation, according to this simplistic way of thinking about sexual perversion, were targeted by religious and later criminal justice authorities as pleasure-inducing, non-procreative and therefore unnatural and sinful because they breached "a basic divine commandment".[9] Engaging in such forms of non-procreative sexual behaviour identified one as a sinner in need of punishment.

However, a re-reading of history, influenced by the work of Michel Foucault, offers a different story about sex and sexuality. It has been argued that "the West inherited an amorphous set of sexual categories which, although making sharp distinctions between the characteristics associated with men and women, assumed that sexual desire could be directed toward a range of objects".[10] Moreover, many acts were sinful – sodomy, pride, gluttony, masturbation – and while they may have been admonished in different ways, "all sin was part of a continuum of transgressions of which each individual man and woman necessarily partook".[11] Questions asked by priests at confession "covered such diverse elements" as slaying of men, lying, use of magic, and misuse of animals – sins concerned with a range of sinful behaviour and not focused solely on sex.[12] It was only with the decline of humoral understandings of medicine and body functionality, between 1670 and 1820 (see chapter 4), that the idea of a natural sexual differentiation between men and women was conceived. In fact, it was only from the late eighteenth century that it was considered normal for men and women to find each other "naturally attractive".[13] With this way of thinking about the sexes came different discourses about sex and sexuality.

More specifically, sex became equated for the first time with genital contact. This is in contrast to previous understandings of sex, most prominent at the end of the seventeenth century, where sex began with the kiss. According to Hitchcock,[14] sexual activity was characterized by "mutual masturbation, much kissing and fondling and long hours spent in mutual touching, but very little penile/vaginal penetration – at least before marriage". As we noted in chapter 4, sexual activity becomes more and more about the penis during the eighteenth and nineteenth centuries, with all other activities associated with sex relegated to "foreplay". This also supports the ways in which sexual regulation shifted over this time, with increased policing of heterosexual sex and concerns over loss of virginity and unwanted pregnancies for women.[15]

This is even more interesting if we consider the very different issues of prostitution and rape. At the beginning of the eighteenth century, to be called a whore "brought into question one's honesty, probity and personal ability as much as one's sexual behaviour".[16] As discussed in more detail in chapter 9, attempts to regulate this morally inappropriate sexual behaviour was a task fraught with danger. In the tenth century, for example, those to be banished for their crimes included "wizards, sorcerers, perjurers, conspirators to murder and horewenan, which included whores, fornicators and adulterers".[17] Nine hundred years later, the Vagrancy (England) Act of 1822 often classified vagrants, professional beggars, cheats and thieves as well as "any woman who yields to her passions and loses her virtue" as prostitutes.[18] The difficulty of accurately identifying whores was partly due to the way in which such behaviour was understood as an "individual moral failure". As we discussed in chapter 4, women were believed to be more lustful and physically desirous of sex than men, from whom they gained the hot and dry essence of male semen. "It was not their participation in illegal sex which put them beyond the pale of normal society but that their circumstances proved their own lack of moral worth."[19] Thus they could be confused with beggars, thieves and adulterers, whose sinful actions also indicated a lack of moral worth.

However, over the course of the eighteenth century, the idea of the prostitute was re-created from one of individual moral failure to that of a victim of seduction. Due in large part to the different understandings of male and female sexuality that emerged during this time, specifically, that women's capacity to conceive was not linked to their sexual pleasure, men were given the active part, naturally speaking, in sex. "The stereotype of seduction placed new onus on male activity and female passivity."[20] In the space of a century, women went from being lustful and full of barely controlled desire, to being sexually numb and passive. In contrast, men, who had begun the century thinking that they could easily control their sexual desires, "due to their greater rationality and mental strength", and that they had a duty to do so, "ended the period being told that their sexual desires were largely beyond their control".[21]

In such a context, the sin of rape can also be re-imagined. In the eighteenth century, rape went from being seen as equivalent to other forms of violent crime, to a uniquely horrible event. The events that led to this change are similar, and related, to the shift in understanding of prostitution. As Hitchcock notes, sexually explicit accounts of rape and sodomy in the Old Bailey Sessions Papers, for example, formed a prominent site for the discussion of sex in eighteenth-century public culture. Moreover, the vast majority of men and women would have felt it appropriate to read this material, with the brutal details which it inevitably included considered to be the "common coin of everyday conversation for both sexes".[22] However, by the end of the eighteenth century, by arguing that women in public were potential victims of rape, due in part to the new understanding that male sexuality was "out of control", women were encouraged to be fearful of rape "and it was justified to keep women off the streets in order to protect them".[23] This shift occurred despite there being no evidence that the number or brutality of rapes had increased, and is accompanied by the suggestion that women were more in fear of straight violence than sexual attack or rape at this time.[24]

Thus the context of sex and sexuality prior to the nineteenth century offers very different ways of thinking about appropriate sexual behaviour. The relation between privacy and sex is a case in point. As we saw in chapter 3, where we now take for granted the house as a space enclosing a single family unit, most previous historical periods saw many people sharing the private space of the home as an economic necessity. Hawkes[25] also notes that it was not until the late seventeenth century that bedrooms came to be defined as private spaces, and only then in the more elite homes of the wealthy. Before this time, bedrooms were "a public space, rather like a sitting room in modern households". Moreover, sharing a bed was not confined to sexual partners. A seventeenth-century rape trial details this point, among others, very nicely.

According to Naphy,[26] in 1613, Georgeo Aricogue claimed that she had been raped by Guillaume Clemencat. The facts of the case are as follows: one evening a man, later identified as Clemencat, came to the bed of Georgeo and they had sex without a word. The man then left the room and did not return. When Georgeo asked her husband the next morning if he had a break from guard duty the previous night and he had not, she became alarmed. Initially she thought that her brother-in-law had accidentally got into the wrong bed, but careful questioning at a family meeting showed this was not the case. When the same man tried the ruse the next night, she recognized him by his clothes and cried out. He fled, but not before he was recognized.

At the trial, it was discovered that Clemencat had indeed entered the bed of Georgeo, knowing full well that her husband was on guard duty. However, it was also revealed during the trial by Susanne le Maistre, a friend of Georgeo, that the following day, Georgeo had admitted to her that she had sex three times the previous evening with a mystery man. Moreover, she had realized that it was not her husband because this man's penis was much larger and was in fact bigger than anyone else she knew. Despite this, the court accepted Georgeo's version of events and Clemencat was banished.

What can we infer from this case of rape in the seventeenth century? Conjugal sex was often silent and almost fully clothed, for one thing, but perhaps more importantly, the fact that her brother-in-law may have accidentally wandered into the wrong bed during the night and had sex with the wrong woman did not appear to surprise anyone. The subsequent shift towards thinking about the bedroom as a private space culminated in new ways of thinking about and regulating sexual activity in the nineteenth century – recall the increased concern over incest discussed in chapter 3, especially within the overcrowded dwellings of the newly urbanized working class. However, the main outcome of positioning a sexual crime as an individual moral failing was that it was not possible to do anything other than punish the indiscretion once it was brought to light. If immoral sexual desire was inherent in all of us, how did one identify the dangerous individual and prevent them from reoffending?

Dangerousness and incapacitation

In 1650 in Massachusetts, a young man by the name of Samuel Terry distressed his neighbours by masturbating in public. He received several lashes on the back to dissuade him from repeating the spectacle, but in 1661 endured another punishment – a fine of four pounds – for indulging in pre-marital intercourse. Finally, in 1673, the court fined Terry and eight other men for performing an "immodest and beastly" play. However, despite this history of sexual offences, a sinner such as Samuel Terry still commanded respect amongst his peers. He served as town constable, and was entrusted by the Court with the custody of another man's infant son. It seemed that "as long as he accepted punishment for his transgressions, he remained a citizen of good standing".[27]

What this example demonstrates is that, while the criminal justice system processed many sex crimes during this time,[28] "there was no sense of the sex criminal as a distinct or especially menacing category of malefactor".[29] The momentous shift which reconceptualized those who committed a prohibited sexual act to a new category of person – someone who had an inner compulsion to violate the innate laws of sex – began with the publication of *Psychopathia Sexualis* by Richard von Krafft-Ebing in 1886.[30] This move by medicine and science into the sexual arena defined and located the boundaries of normal sexual behaviour through the discovery of perversion, for without the identification of perversion, there could be no normality.[31] For the first time, a person who committed a sexually perverse act was perceived of as pathologically driven to do so because of biological and psychological propensities. No longer was an immoral desire inherent in all of us; instead, the sex offender was "essentially supernaturally dangerous and contaminating to the idealized social body".[32]

This did not mean, however, that religious ideas about a "lack of moral worth" shifted out of focus. Rather, the immorality of certain sexual acts was superimposed on legal codes,[33] and governing authorities continued to exercise "wide latitude in penalizing individuals guilty not of serious crime but of moral or sexual unortho-doxy".[34] According to Morrison, such legislation in the nineteenth century "prohibited a few truly dangerous and incurable offenders from acting, but under the same 'sex offense' category, it also outlawed homosexuality, public displays of nudity, obscenity (including pornography), and risqué sexual proposals".[35]

By forging the old discourse of immorality with the new one of uncontrollability, the concept of the sexual psychopath emerged as a form of criminal identity. Scientific understandings of sex offending as being triggered by an internal psychological imbalance married well with the long-standing assumptions that sexual transgressions were the result of a lack of moral worth. These shifts in understanding came about within an increasing raft of psychological and medical discourses which con-ceptualized the sex offender as a specific type of person whose "deviant acts were symptoms indicating underlying medical or biological flaws ... conditions that demanded treatment or incapacitation".[36]

Legislation following this line of reasoning saw the first sexual psychopath laws being adopted in the late 1930s in the United States. This legislation made it possible to civilly commit identified sexual psychopaths for indeterminate periods in psychiatric institutions, based on the decision of a panel of psychological experts. As the most severe type of sex offender, sexual psychopaths were positioned as predisposed to commit further sexual crimes due to their abnormal state of being.[37] Freedman notes how the wording of this legislation was vital in enabling this process: "the sexual psychopath was someone whose 'utter lack of power to control his sexual impulses' made him 'likely to attack ... the objects of his uncontrolled and uncontrollable desires'".[38] As a consequence, the term "dangerous" shifted from being an adjective to working as a noun – "dangerousness" – that described and defined the parameters of a "dangerous person".[39] Just as Foucault observed about the homosexual in the nineteenth century, so the dangerous sex offender also became "a personage, a past, a case history, and a childhood, in addition to being a type of life, a life form, and a morphology, with an indiscreet anatomy and possibly a mysterious physiology".[40]

However, this identification of the dangerous sex offender, their incapacitation in psychiatric hospitals and their psychological treatment was limited to those who had already committed dangerous sexual acts. "In assessing dangerousness, the past of an individual is of interest primarily for the purpose of predicting and controlling his future behaviour."[41] By treating dangerousness as an internal quality, it limited any possibility of establishing and maintaining an effective policy of prevention in the larger society. After all, "one could only hope to prevent violent acts committed by those whom one had already diagnosed as dangerous ... and such diagnoses ... can only be carried out on individual patients one by one".[42] Psychiatrists could not diagnose accurately, and effectively neutralize, dangerousness in every single case – short of confining massive numbers of people on the smallest suspicion of danger. Moreover, "harmless today, they may be dangerous tomorrow".[43]

Once the focus of the criminal justice system moved from the crime to the criminal, the task was to reveal the impetus for dangerousness in the body of the individual. With the increasing medicalization of criminal danger, it was only a matter of time before "any criminal could be treated as potentially pathological, any minor infraction as suspect, any variation an antecedent".[44]

Risk and public safety

The popularity of the idea of risk in criminal justice is precisely due to its capacity for prediction, and such prediction is possible only because risk is associated with a given population, not an individual. Rather than a clinical diagnosis, the analysis of risk offers a statistical probability. Since risk becomes calculable only when spread over a population, it has meaning only when located within a population about which a significant amount of knowledge has been gained. Moreover, the implication of managing populations "at risk" is much more significant than simply relabelling those previously defined as dangerousness. Although dangerousness may be operationalized through risk, what appears as a small semantic change actually signals an important expansion in the possibilities of governmental regulation.[45] Consider the following two examples as a case in point.

In 2003, the *Dangerous Prisoners (Sexual Offenders) Act* came into force in Queensland, Australia, and enabled criminal justice authorities for the first time to detain indefinitely sex offenders who are assessed to be manifestly and continually dangerous. This is not uncommon legislation. In the United States, for example, a prediction of "future dangerousness" is the basis for indefinite treatment and detainment in specialized treatment facilities such as the Wisconsin Sex Offender Treatment Facility, where dangerous sex offenders are moved once they have completed their prison sentence. Such civil commitment laws are now operating in thirty-nine states across the country. Similarly, in the UK the *Criminal Justice Act 2003* enables those assessed with future dangerousness to be detained after completing the sentence for their initial sexual crime.[46] These various pieces of legislation, some civil and some criminal, predict the future dangerousness of a convicted sex offender via an individual clinical diagnosis of paraphilia, personality disorder or mental abnormality.[47]

In contrast, the *Sex Offenders Bill*, passed in the UK in 1997 and then subsumed under the *Sexual Offences Act* of 2003, required all those convicted of Schedule 1 sex offences, upon release from prison, to notify the police in person of any change in address within fourteen days. Conviction of serious sex offences of more than thirty months' imprisonment meant a lifetime requirement to notify the police, while lesser sentences required decreased periods of time on the register. Most interesting for this discussion was the inclusion on the register of those who had only ever been cautioned with a sex offence, while those offences excluded from the requirement to register included bigamy, abduction, soliciting by a man, incest by a woman and indecent exposure. By 2003, there were more than 15,000 individuals recorded on the register.[48] In this second example, there is no clinical diagnosis of dangerousness. In fact, these prisoners have been released precisely because they are not perceived to be dangerous in the future. They are, however, a population deemed "at risk" (of both reoffending and being offended against).

Thus, while selective incapacitation ensures that dangerous offenders are expunged from public space in ways reminiscent of what Foucault calls "the great confinement",[49] sex offenders who complete their sentences but are not predicted to be dangerous still face a range of restrictions on their movements in public space. Depending on the local legislation, sex offenders can be subject to a range of techniques that "mark" their bodies as sites of governance in public spaces. This can be enabled by community-notification statutes that employ strategies such as leaflet drops, community meetings, media reporting of addresses, and telephone hotlines, to name just a few.[50]

All these approaches have been trialled in various parts of the western world, and are a clear attempt to manage the risk posed by sex offenders by making them visible in public space. Such visibility becomes a powerful regulatory mechanism that surveils the spaces sex offenders inhabit in their local communities. Indeed, in some approaches, the general public become a form of "moral police", ensuring that sex offenders are kept at an appropriate distance from (morally) respectable society. Interestingly, community-notification techniques like these have been found to be ineffective in shoring up the safety of the community,[51] while more telling is research demonstrating how the stigma of community-notification processes "may inadvertently increase the likelihood of recidivism among some sex offenders … by making it more difficult to achieve meaningful stability in important areas of their lives and facilitate positive relationships".[52] Gaining and maintaining employment is also seriously hampered by employers' attitudes to known sex offenders.[53] Moreover, the moral panic underpinning community notification has been found to increase the probability of recidivism.

However, the rise of risk did not supplant the older idea of dangerousness, but rather widened its ambit to a larger population, much in the same way as dangerousness simply worked with the older model of immorality. With sex offender registers in their various guises, we have a form of regulation of an at-risk population which sits easily with religious ideas of moral worth and fear of dangerous individuals. Perhaps more interestingly, given our previous discussion about the changing nature of both sex and sexuality, in the exponential rise of sex offender legislation we also see an outcome of the shift to passive female sexuality and active male sexuality. It will not be surprising to note, for example, that it is men who are the most likely to be identified as either dangerous sex offenders requiring indeterminate incapacitation and/or "at-risk" sex offenders placed on public registers, while women and female children are most likely identified as victims of such offences.[54]

The moral panic about children and sex discussed in some detail in chapters 2 and 3 is also relevant to current ideas about the risk of sex offenders. Much more than property offences, or even physical assaults, "sex offences against persons are considered to be violations that damage the very core of victims".[55] The more sacred, pure or innocent the victim, the more profane the violation and the offender. Children are the most innocent group in contemporary society, and because of this are also perceived as the most vulnerable, out of all proportion to reality. For example, at the end of the twentieth century, the number of sex offences against adults in the UK was reported as 37,492, of which 6000 were rapes and the remainder indecent assaults. In contrast, indecent assaults against girls under sixteen numbered 2116, and against boys, 476.[56]

Despite these low numbers, much of the impetus for the increased public surveillance of sex offenders is motivated by calls for public safety, especially of children. Residency restrictions exemplify how governmental authorities maintain moral and spatial distance between children and sex offenders by legislating the physical distances sex offenders may reside from spaces where children congregate. This may include proximity to schools, child care centres, shopping centres, playgrounds, skating rinks, neighbourhood centres, gymnasiums and youth centres. However, if we consider for a moment the number of child care centres alone in a local community, we begin to understand how residency restrictions work to further isolate and exclude sex offenders from society. An American study by Zandbergen and Hart[57] used geographical information system data to calculate how much housing would be unavailable to sex offenders in the area of Orange County, Florida, due to residence restrictions. They found "23% of the 137,944 properties zoned for residential use were located within 1000 feet of schools and 64% fell within 2500 feet, reducing the number of available residences to 106,888 and 50,108 respectively".

Other studies have noted the continuum of negative outcomes for the lives of sex offenders, from lack of access to housing to living homeless long term.[58] Perhaps the most powerful element of residency restriction legislation, though, is that it can apply for between ten and fifteen years after the sex offender has completed their sentence and been released from prison. Moreover, given that many people are defined as sex offenders for very minor crimes, including public exposure, or conducting a consensual sexual relationship with a person who is only just under the age of consent, such management techniques seem harsh in the extreme. This has been exacerbated through the use of global positioning systems (GPS), which ensure perpetual surveillance of sex offenders.[59] Such mechanisms have been implemented in various parts of the United States, Britain and Australia, for example, through electronic monitoring anklets and bracelets. These have already proved useful in serving breach notices related to this legislation and in having sex offenders re-incarcerated. More importantly, though, these forms of regulation restrict free movement to the point where regulation becomes "punishment in the absence of any evidence of wrongdoing".[60]

Conclusion

This chapter has charted how we have come to think about sex offenders as morally perverted and dangerous predators, a personhood that legitimates their enduring regulation in public space. In this contemporary context, an offender such as Arthurs is legitimately incarcerated for life on the basis that he is too morally and psychologically different to be able to coexist safely with the rest of society. Should Arthurs ever be released, his movements and time will inevitably be surveilled for the remainder of his life. His is marked as a body of sin and danger, one that reflects and justifies public panic and demands to ensure child sexual safety. That our contemporary perceptions about sex offenders have developed only recently, based on changes in understandings of sex and public space, illustrates just how intolerant society is of sexual deviance, regardless of whether there is any real basis for concern. In chapter 7, we explore public discourses on other kinds of sexual deviance in order to demonstrate how contradictory these discourses are to contemporary perceptions that we, as an advanced and sexually experienced society, entertain a more liberal attitude towards sexuality.

7

SEXUALITY

Introduction

Discourses about sex and sexuality seem to have become more public and, in many ways, more acceptable in recent years. We have become much more open to discussing varieties of sex and sexual activity, and to pondering over our relevant appetites, insufficiencies and achievements to the point where prominent newspapers now have resident sexologists to answer our questions, and sex blogging on the internet has become almost passé. Indeed, the recent media picnic over a music video by pop divas Lady Gaga and Beyoncé featuring lesbian tropes emphasize the ravenousness with which we digest apparent sexual deviance. In chapter 5 we examined the concept of moral space and how categories of indecency and offence have developed over time. In this chapter, we continue to explore this concept with particular reference to "deviant" sexualities. Public discourses about sex have also changed remarkably over recent years, and this chapter analyses the ways in which public discourses and public spaces have opened up to other sexualities in ways that appear quite liberating for the non-heterosexual. Indeed, the effects of such public discourses have been largely positive with respect to adult entertainment and other forms of sexual commerce, and we analyse those effects in chapter 9. In this chapter, however, we explore the effects of public discourses on sexual identity, and how the opening up of public spaces and public discourses may in fact have contributed to the continued marginalization of sexual minorities. We question the liberating effects of the current discursive preoccupation with sex and sexualities, and suggest that these discourses serve to define and regulate non-heterosexualities more than ever before. Indeed, we argue that it is only in the context of shame that such discourses can be considered transgressive and therefore evident of real resistance.

Deviant sexualities

The latter point was made evident at a recent afternoon symposium on "Sex blogging, gender, and sexual subcultures", held at a well-known university campus in

London. The aim of the seminar was to challenge "traditional" sex blogging. Blogging is the short name for a web log – an online journal of sorts, resembling a diary, but often far more complex. Given the resource capabilities of the internet, contemporary blogs can include everything from advertising and recommendations for other websites, to archival resources and community options for comment and "following". Sex blogging in particular has become popular over the past several years, with a proliferation of online journals aimed at both exposé and genuine discussion. Several of the most prominent authors have made news headlines by blogging about sex work, sado-masochism, group sex and other non-normative sex practices.[1] But sex blogging is not the topic we want to discuss in this chapter – that we will leave until chapter 8. The point of interest in this example is the seminar itself.

Three papers were scheduled over the afternoon, one of them by an actual sex worker and blogger, Kitty Stryker, who became well known in the mainstream media in 2008–09 around the same time that sex blogging came to the attention of the general public. Ostensibly, her paper was a theorizing of the nature of sex work and "kink", drawing on Stryker's experience as a professional dominatrix both in California and, more recently, in London. The other papers were more scholarly, the first a general analysis of what was labelled "traditional" sex blogging, the second a discussion of another kink-oriented sex blog by a supposedly female author going by the name of Bitchy Jones. Both of these papers drew on a variety of feminist and queer theory,[2] illustrated by graphic quotes from the sex blogs in question.

What was interesting about these papers, and the seminar itself, was not only the ease with which the topics of sex blogging, sex work, lesbianism and sado-masochism were discussed, but the fact that any sex blogging could be regarded as traditional. A decade ago, discussions of sex work were focused around feminist-inspired arguments of the exploitation of women, or public health warnings against the physical, mental and emotional impact of sex work on its "victims" – be they prostitutes or clients.[3] Public discourses on sex itself were confined to news reports of rape or other sexual violence, the moral depravity of prostitution and paedophilia, child sexual abuse, or education about safe sex. It is a turning point in the development of such discourses that a group of British academics can gather under the self-styled label of "critical sexology" to discuss sexuality and non-normative sexual practices and identities, that they can discuss these issues in the public forum offered by the university, and that they can be funded to do so. Similarly, the public acceptance and even celebration of sex blogging speaks of a giant leap forward in social attitudes towards sex outside marriage and beyond heterosexuality. That women such as Abby Lee, author of "Girl With a One-track Mind",[4] or sex workers such as Kitty Stryker, who blogs under the title of "PurrVersatility",[5] can achieve cult status for blogging about their sexual exploits, suggests that social attitudes towards sex and sexuality have come a long way. Indeed, the public labelling of some kinds of sex blogging as "traditional" suggests that sex of the vanilla, one-on-one, heterosexual, even commercial variety is somewhat passé.

In her critical sexology seminar paper titled "Raunch vs prude: contemporary sex blogs and erotic memoirs by women",[6] Kaye Mitchell offers a humorous, almost scathing analysis of traditional sex blogs such as Lee's and high-class sex-worker Belle de Jour's,[7] arguing that they are not nearly radical or transgressive enough to warrant all the recent attention – that their protagonists' vanilla sexploits place women squarely back into stereotypes that not only cause harm through an overbearingly sexist zeitgeist, and that even their forays into lesbian and group sex merely tip their hat to other sexualities, without actually coming to grips with what it means to have "real lesbian sex". Meg Barker and Rosalind Gill followed with a paper discussing sexual subjectivity via the vehicle of a blog on bondage/domination/sado-masochism (BDSM) by Bitchy Jones.[8] For Barker and Gill, this blogger's criticism of "traditional" BDSM was nothing short of a revelation in the way it subverted stereotypical dominant–submissive roles and identities. Finally, Kitty Stryker discussed the intricacies of being a "femdom" and a "prodom",[9] while shunning the traditional stereotype of the cat-suited, spiked-heeled, male fantasy dominatrix. Needless to say, the audience – consisting mostly of white, upper-class, educated, female academics – was enthralled.

Much discussion followed this learned exchange, and we and our colleagues listened with rapt attention to calls for a more transgressive discourse on, and practice of, sex and sexuality than was currently offered by traditional sex blogging and vanilla sex. Clearly, the audience was well at ease with the sex talk, the references to various kinks, the ceiling-high images of sex workers and their clients that flashed across the slide presentation, and the colourful use of "fuck", "arse-fuck" and "mother-fuck" throughout the presentations. Surely this group, in this public setting, is providing as transgressive an exchange, as radical a challenge, to the closeted and stymied sexual discourses traditionally on offer in the wider context of society as could possibly be imagined. When Kaye Mitchell giggles that her research is becoming "more queer" by the day, and that traditional sex bloggers have no idea how "real" lesbians have sex (intimating – if not screaming outright – that she does), doesn't that tell us that we've reached a true turning point in how we as a public think and talk about sex? When Kitty Stryker casually remarks that she is a "queer woman" who has been hurting men sexually for money for some ten years, and shows us pictures, members of the audience nod appreciatively, because isn't this just what being sexually liberated is really all about?

In the 1980s and 1990s, some lesbian feminists argued that women were not merely passive receptors of sex and violence, nor merely victims of male pornification; that women could also be producers of sexual desire and titillation and consumers of sexual pleasure.[10] These women argued that it was possible – indeed, it was happening – that women themselves could be sexual subjects in ways that were both empowering of them as women, and liberating of them sexually. Lesbian feminists of this period subverted sexual objectification, turned it on its head, and used it for their own pleasure, as a way of both thumbing their noses at heteronormativity and heterosexism, and demonstrating the way in which women could also participate as subjects in the sexual landscape. These manifestations of non-normative sexuality were transgressive because they challenged norms of the time surrounding gender, sexuality, desire and subjectivity, and opened up a broader discussion about lesbians and the role of sex in women's lives – topics that had previously been silenced, rendered invisible.

One might be tempted to think that such critical sexologists are furthering this transgressive discourse on female sexuality and subjectivity, and indeed, the fact that such discourses as those offered in the sex blogging seminar are occupying public spaces and accepted as part of the academic landscape suggests that attitudes are broadening to some extent. But simply blogging about sexuality, or discussing kinks and lesbian sex, does not necessarily make for subversive discourse, although one might be forgiven for thinking it so in the context of the white, female, upper-class academic group that made up that particular critical sexology seminar. These collectively attractive, well-heeled, confident and admirable women were certainly cutting-edge in terms of their particular assemblage. But it bears asking how the critical discussion of "femdom" and "femsub" speaks to the experience of, for example, the lesbian couple who are vilified for their sexuality by the other occupants of their block of council flats, or what the proper knowledge of lesbian sex or kink means for the frightened young woman who feels alienated by her gender. Talking about sex, queerness and bondage does not make for liberation *per se*. Indeed, we suggest that such talk serves to further the heteronormative ideal – and thus to silence real difference – rather than subvert it.

It has become almost *de rigeur* to be broad-minded about sex and sexuality in our twenty-first-century western society. But this broad-mindedness does not consist of being open to real difference at all. Rather, it employs images and ideas of "deviant" sexualities for the purposes of titillation and sexual provocation. Look at the number of music videos currently depicting pretty, male-fantasy lesbians with locked lips and all-but-bare torsos, writhing in simulated passion. Katy Perry[11] claims to have kissed a girl and liked it, but all we see on the music video is images of corseted, voluptuous, very heteronormative young women smiling seductively towards us as Katy sings about being "naughty" and "caught up in the moment". Sibling duo TaTu[12] have also been using this same deviance-as-seduction, posing in music videos as lovers to the delight of both male and female audiences. And popular music legend Madonna has been doing it for years. Clearly, intimations of lesbianism are sexy to a broadly heterosexual audience that is tired of the same old male-on-female seductive images. Indeed, a trip to any trendy urban club will find women locked in amorous embrace for the benefit of the panting male audience. These "barsexuals",[13] so named for the fact that they are demonstrating difference only in the context of the bar and to excite their boyfriends, are about as heteronormative as one can get. Try confronting a similar audience with two big, butch lesbians in a similar position, and see what happens. Our beautiful, upper-class, white, female, critical sexologists might also be accused of succumbing to the heteronormative push to employ deviance as a way of silencing real difference and making it invisible. Almost to a person, these women were coiffed, heavily made-up, high-heeled, and dressed in flattering feminine outfits. When their bright red lips form around words like "arse-fuck" and "femdom", they serve the same purpose, it might be argued, as the pretty barsexuals or male-fantasy lesbians of music videos, in using deviance and apparent difference to appear transgressive while in fact setting in stone dominant paradigms of sexuality and sexual attractiveness, and thereby rendering invisible yet again the kinds of real difference experienced in the everyday lives of "deviants" everywhere.

In exploring the invisibility of deviant sexualities, we by no means suggest that society is unaware of the existence of gay, lesbian, transgender, intersex or queer individuals. Indeed, such deviance has been a thorn in the side of western civilization for many centuries, and only recently has being "queer"[14] been decriminalized – though it is still regulated. Many non-western countries continue to enforce sodomy laws, some punishable by death (for example, at the time of writing, in Iran, Mauritania, Saudi Arabia, Sudan, the United Arab Emirates and Yemen), others by prison for life (Barbados, Bangladesh, Guyana, Maldives, Sierra Leone and Uganda). In Australia, the last revoking of sodomy laws occurred as late as 1997, in Tasmania. In the State of Queensland, for example, Section 208 of the Criminal Code still punishes sodomy for those under eighteen years of age, with a penalty of up to fourteen years' imprisonment. The fact that people who identify as non-heterosexual are now – slowly – being given the same rights as heterosexuals suggests that society is indeed aware, and becoming more tolerant, of sexual deviance. A 2008 Galaxy poll, for example, reported that over 60 per cent of Queenslanders support civil unions for gay and lesbian couples.[15] Across Australia, this figure rises to almost 80 per cent.[16] And yet, in February 2009, legislation was passed in Queensland framing new adoption laws that nevertheless prohibit adoption by same-sex couples. These seeming contradictions illustrate the often ambivalent attitudes towards sexual minorities. What is more, they point up the ways in which deviance is driven from public spaces that are essentially and solely dedicated to heterosexual and family pursuits. The criminalization of sodomy itself is a regulation of sexual geography which ensures that what offends the heteronormative is either abolished or, at the very least, relegated to deviant space well away from traditional public areas.

Regulating sexualities

USLegal, Inc.[17] defines sodomy as a "crime against nature", suggesting that what is natural is heterosexual, despite the fact that sodomy may also be committed upon women by men and – with a little help – vice versa. The overarching meaning of a crime against nature is that it is not committed for the purposes of procreation or male–female marital bonding. It is defined in one US state law as "Any act of sexual gratification between persons not married to each other involving the sex organs of one person and the mouth or anus of another."

The first sodomy laws date back to the Middle Assyrian Law Codes of 1075, which were military codes prohibiting men from having penetrative sex with one another. Not long after, the Romans enacted *Lex Scantinia*, a set of laws restricting – but not prohibiting – sodomy, where the use of slaves for sexual purposes was permitted "as long as the slave was on the receiving end".[18] Western laws are based on Judaeo-Christian principles derived from the Old Testament *Book of Leviticus*, the King James version of which states "Thou shalt not lie with mankind, as with womankind: it is abomination" (18: 22). In England, Henry VIII passed the *Buggery Act of 1533*, making sodomy an offence punishable by hanging until 1861. Sir William Blackstone's eighteenth-century *Commentaries on the Laws of England* described the crime of sodomy as an "abominable and detestable crime against nature", though nowhere were the details of what actually constituted the act of sodomy clearly outlined.[19] Although the death penalty was eventually dropped, sodomy continued to be a crime against nature in the United Kingdom until 1957, when the Wolfenden Report argued that "homosexual behaviour between consenting adults should no longer be a criminal offence".[20] However, while many western governments proceeded to decriminalize "homosexual behaviour" in general, many retained their laws against the act of sodomy itself.

Australia inherited Britain's laws in 1788 and operated under similar legislation until 1972, when the Dunstan Labor government introduced a "consenting adults in private" defence in South Australia.[21] The state's sodomy law was duly repealed in 1975, triggering a spate of similar reforms throughout the other states, with, as mentioned above, Tasmania being the last to conform. In the United States, however, it wasn't until 2003 that sodomy was finally decriminalized after the Supreme Court case of *Lawrence* v. *Texas* ruled that "state laws criminalizing private, non-commercial sexual activity between consenting adults at home on the grounds of morality are unconstitutional since there is insufficient justification for intruding into people's liberty and privacy". Thus, while states such as Alabama and Mississippi continue to list sodomy laws on their books, it is doubtful that any challenge to them would be defeated in a court of law. Nevertheless, recent news footage from Uganda covering a campaign to bring in the death penalty for sodomy highlights the very precarious status of homosexuality and acts of sodomy on the world stage.[22] Where the western world has appeared to move forward with respect to recognizing non-heterosexualities, other nations remain seemingly fixed in their view of homosexual acts as crimes against nature and humankind.

As we can see from this brief legislative history, sexuality has been regulated largely through the criminalization of certain acts. Interestingly, such legislation was always directed at acts involving penal penetration, and consequently lesbianism has never been formally regulated or criminalized. But legal regulation of sodomy is only half the story of the regulation of deviant sexualities. From the mid-nineteenth century, medical and legal discourses not only started to identify more and more inappropriate sexual relations – think back to chapters 3 and 4 – but also started the process of linking certain forms of deviant sexual behaviour with specific deviant sexual identities.[23] Hence the category of "homosexual" was created and, by extension, the category of "heterosexual". This distinction positioned the heterosexual as the norm, and the homosexual as a pathological or deviant other, in need of some form of correction. Those who failed to conform to the norm were diagnosed, labelled and then "treated for" or "reformed of" their sexual deviance.[24] From this period, the focus of social regulation was not on acts themselves, but rather on distinct *kinds of person*. Sexuality became tied to a person's identity, and the idea that people have an essential sexuality (and, indeed, an essential self) has been widespread ever since.

Homosexuality has become tied to identity to such an extent that it is seen to form the individual's essential nature; indeed, the homosexual individual just *is* their sexuality.[25] Modern individuals are increasingly governed by, and come to govern themselves through, these standards and categories. Those defined as homosexual understand themselves by using these discourses on sexuality, recognizing that they "have" a sexuality, and that this defines them as a person. These are produced and reinforced in established sites such as the social sciences, medicine and psychiatry.[26] This creation of authoritative categories of sexuality, the normalization of heterosexuality, and the subsequent casting of homosexuality in opposition to heterosexuality, has produced numerous contradictory and condemnatory discourses. At the same time as homosexuality is not to be spoken of, it is also the object of discourses that name, categorize, judge and speak on behalf of those who fall within its purview.[27] These discourses, which Sedgwick so neatly describes as the "epistemology of the closet",[28] serve to silence and to govern non-heterosexualities, as well as to essentialize them.

This particular approach to sexuality has provided the basis for innumerable scholarly analyses of the ways in which non-heterosexual (and even heterosexual) identities are constructed through interaction with these discourses on sexuality, as well as how these identities are continually performed. It has also led to similar research on other supposedly "natural" aspects of identities, such as gender and race. In many respects, this approach to understanding sexuality and sexual identity as positioned through discourse underpins this book, interested as it is in teasing out the way that these understandings of essentialized human nature – and, by extension, sexuality – feature as part of social interactions and discussions, and the effect this has on the way people interact with non-heterosexualities and even on how they understand their "own" sexuality.

Homo-queasiness and homophobia

Although discriminatory attitudes towards homosexuality have received some much-needed attention in recent years, and sodomy has been largely decriminalized throughout the western world, there still remain many laws that exclude and/or discriminate against same-sex couples, transgender and intersexed individuals. Despite these decriminalizations, homosexual individuals still remain "othered" in society. Recent research suggests that even in largely tolerant societies, where non-heterosexualities are more or less accepted, a large number of people are still what can be called "homo-queasy", if not outright homophobic. Homo-queasy is the term employed by the Gay & Lesbian Alliance Against Defamation (GLAAD) to describe attitudes that poke fun at homosexuality, albeit often good-naturedly. Research by Hayes and Ball[29] applied this conceptualization to research on attitudes towards gay and lesbian peers among a group of Australian university students and discovered that, while most students expressed support for queer issues and individuals, they "wouldn't want to be one". Students understand the queer individual as outside the mainstream – as "other" – and, in the same breath as they claim to support gay rights, comment that the thought of gay sex is disturbing. It is clear that more widespread discourses on heterosexuality and homosexuality as distinct identity categories, and the social acceptance of the normality of heterosexuality and the deviance or otherness of homosexuality, informs students' acceptance and understanding of sexuality. In many cases, this creates an undercurrent of fear, discomfort or ambivalence.[30] The students themselves may be prepared to accept gay-identifying individuals, but they could also see that many others in society are not so accepting. They were able to recognize that homophobia is a fact of life in a society built on powerful heteronormative discourses. It is this acknowledgment that creates the framework for the continuation of gay identities and gay discourses as other, and therefore deviant.

This homo-queasiness appears to pervade western society in general, even in the face of campaigns supporting equal rights. Certainly, the rights of same-sex couples are becoming more of an issue. The UK *Civil Partnership Act 2004*, for example, allows same-sex couples to register their partnership and thereby obtain similar rights to heterosexual married couples. That same year, the UK also passed the *Gender Recognition ACT 2004*, allowing "transsexual" individuals to change their legal gender.[31] In New Zealand, both same-sex and heterosexual couples can choose to register a civil union, which entitles couples to the same rights as married couples, although only heterosexual couples also have the choice of traditional marriage. And in the USA, several states, including Connecticut, Iowa, New Jersey and New York, allow same-sex marriage. Other states – Alaska, Alabama, Florida and Indiana, among others, for example – have passed laws specifically banning same-sex marriage, although one state, Massachusetts, has passed legislation that prohibits the banning of marriage between same-sex couples.

In Australia, only the Australian Capital Territory (ACT) has attempted (unsuccessfully) to pass a law to allow civil partnerships. This attempt was defeated by the *Commonwealth Marriage Act 1961*, which was amended to specifically prohibit recognition of same-sex marriage. In other states, same-sex couples are now recognized to the same degree as heterosexual *de facto* couples, often described as "unregistered cohabitation", and a recent Human Rights Commission report, *Same Sex: Same Entitlements*,[32] has resulted in the amendment of eighty-four Commonwealth laws "to eliminate discriminations against same-sex couples and their children". Specific laws amended include those affecting taxation, superannuation, social security and family assistance, aged care, child support and immigration. In addition, formal domestic partnership registries exist in Tasmania, Victoria and the ACT.

When we add all this legislative reform occurring in western nations to our previous observations about public discourses on sex and sexuality, one would think that attitudes towards "deviant" sexualities and same-sex couples have taken a turn for the better. Our critical sexologists can talk about deviance and kink in a public forum virtually without fear of censure, because sex talk is commonplace. Same-sex couples can formally register their union in a variety of nations, because society recognizes that they are moral agents who deserve the same kinds of rights and entitlements as heterosexual couples and families. Pop divas can embrace other women in the public space of the media and barely raise an eyebrow, and even average women can dance up close and sexy in clubs, kiss or go even further, in the knowledge that they will probably not be discriminated against. But if deviant sexualities have really made it into "real" (as opposed to marginalized) public spaces, then how do we account for the still high numbers of hate crimes perpetrated against gay, lesbian and transgender people? Why can two women kiss in a bar unheeded, while two men can't kiss in the street without fear of a bashing? How can a white, upper-class, female academic talk about queer sex and the art of sadism without fear of reproach or even physical harm? Clearly, there is no little discrepancy between the public discourses that allow sex bloggers, academics, pop divas and pretty women in bars licence to be "transgressive" of heterosexual norms, and the other discourses we hear that condemn, discriminate against and threaten the queers and deviants who are objects of street bashings and public ridicule because of their sexuality.

Perhaps the difference can be teased out by examining another set of examples from the media. On 11 October 2009, UK newspaper *The Guardian* reported that Stephen Gately, a prominent musician and singer in the band Boyzone, had died the day before while on holiday in Majorca.[33] Gately had been found that morning by his civil partner, Andrew Cowles, and "Spanish police said there were 'no signs of suspicious circumstances'" surrounding the death.[34] Later, it was revealed that Gately and Cowles had been out at a club the previous evening, had come in late, Gately had fallen into unconsciousness on his couch and apparently suffered a heart attack. Gately had come out as gay some ten years before, and was well known and well loved both by peers in the music world and by his loyal fans, many of whom paid tribute to his fine talents while mourning his loss. The following day, *Daily Mail* journalist Jan Moir wrote a column about Gately's death, the public response to which created a veritable media storm. Moir's article, which was titled "Why there was nothing 'natural' about Stephen Gately's death" (later amended online to read "A strange, lonely and troubling death") provoked public outcry against Moir's apparent homophobia, where she states:

> Hang on a minute. Something is terribly wrong with the way this incident has been shaped and spun into nothing more than an unfortunate mishap on a holiday weekend …
>
> The sugar coating on this fatality is so saccharine-thick that it obscures whatever bitter truth lies beneath. Healthy and fit 33-year-old men do not just climb into their pyjamas and go to sleep on the sofa, never to wake up again.
>
> Whatever the cause of death is, it is not, by any yardstick, a natural one.

The article offers much sly innuendo concerning the circumstances surrounding Gately's death, suggesting that "[o]nce again, under the carapace of glittering, hedonistic celebrity, the ooze of a very different and more dangerous lifestyle has seeped out for all to see".[35] Overnight, there were over 800 comments online, all "overwhelmingly antagonistic"[36] to Moir's article, and a call went out on Twitter for members of the public to complain about Moir's homophobic comments to the relevant media watchdog. Charlie Brooker, a writer for *The Guardian*, commented that "Jan Moir's rant about the Boyzone star Stephen Gately is a gratuitous piece of gay-bashing",[37] receiving over 1000 comments online, most of them in agreement with his condemnation of Moir. Indeed, both public support for Gately and condemnation of Moir were so strong that UK corporation Marks and Spencer pulled all its advertising from the *Daily Mail,* while other companies threatened to do the same. In the face of such scorn, Moir was forced to publish an apology.

Even as this public debate was occurring, however, another gay British man, Ian Baynham, was killed by thugs in Trafalgar Square on 15 October 2009, in what was later described by *The Times* as a "heinous homophobic hate crime". *Times Online*[38] reported:

> Ian Baynham, 62, was walking through Trafalgar Square in Central London with a 30-year-old friend when a woman began shouting homophobic abuse at him.
>
> He went to talk to her but she attacked him and a man with her is said to have punched him to the floor and then kicked him. A second young woman was also involved in the incident.

A little over a month later, statistics from the Crown Prosecutor's Office reported a marked increase in homophobic and transphobic hate crimes in the UK[39] – specifically, a 10 per cent increase over the previous four years. Thus, despite the overwhelming public support for Stephen Gately in the face of homophobic attack, it seems that the statistics show a different story about social attitudes towards gay men and queers in general. Again, we might ask why the public are so well disposed towards deviant sexuality in one situation while maintaining a generally unacceptable level of fear and hatred in another. *The Times* story about Baynham drew eleven comments – quite a difference from the more than 1000 comments in support of Gately just days earlier. We suggest that this discrepancy demonstrates the continued fragility of public attitudes towards deviant sexualities, a fragility that belies the overtly positive public discourses in support of deviance, and provides evidence for the continued marginalization of sexual minorities in our society.

Gately was a highly regarded performer, a member of a very successful boy band of the 1990s and early 2000s. Though not quite achieving the status of Sir Elton John or George Michael, both of whom are well-known gay celebrities in the music world, Gately had achieved the kind of quiet, well-earned status accorded to musicians of reasonable success who had paid their dues and deserved ongoing approbation. He was, first and foremost, a performer – a very successful one – and the fact of his sexuality, though a shock to his fans at his coming out a decade ago, was just a part of a very well-known and well-loved public identity. The status of celebrity in this case appears to outweigh or even negate the deviant sexuality. When Gately came out, he was already a huge success – for that matter, the same is true of both Elton John and George Michael. For these celebrities, coming out was a matter of stating one fact about an identity that was already celebrated, if for other reasons, such as music. Their celebrated status meant there was little, if anything, at stake in their coming out. Indeed, in the entertainment industry, being gay – or lesbian, or bisexual – is more often than not regarded as a lovable quirk, something almost unique that adds a little intrigue to the person. For these men, there is no shame in being gay. Ian Baynham, on the other hand, had no celebrity status to protect him.

The more public an individual's non-sexual identity becomes, it seems, the less they have at stake in revealing any deep, dark secrets about their sexuality – or anything else. We, as a public, are ever-forgiving of the transgressions of celebrities because they fascinate and entertain us, and their lives are more fabulous than we will ever know, raising them above such petty labels as "deviant" – for celebrities, there is no shame in being different.[40] Indeed, it is more often celebrated as yet one more trait to envy in an already fabulous existence. In the context of celebrity, being different is really just another star in the crown.

Dare we say the same about the critical sexologists in our earlier example? While academics in general – sadly – can hardly be regarded as celebrities in any sense of the word, the relevant similarity here lies not in fame or fortune, but in the expression of shame and what is at stake in coming out. Though far from famous, our sexologists present first and foremost as willing participants in the heteronormative world – their transgression (if it can be called that) in terms of sexuality is secondary, a minor element of an overarching identity which sees them construct themselves as women of a certain background, with specific class, speech and modes of dress that locate them squarely within a particular category within that heteronormative world. The physical signifiers they present speak to a conformity that, to some degree, outweighs any transgressions of speech and act. In other words, these women have very little at stake in coming out as sexual "deviants". Here, again, there is no shame involved in identifying a penchant for lesbian sex or BDSM – indeed, such characteristics are regarded as titillating elements of a personal identity that transgresses just enough to be juicy, while maintaining enough semblance of propriety to get away with it.

Conclusion

In this chapter, we suggest that the moral geography of sexuality acknowledges the shame involved in being deviant and marginalizes those who continue to transgress heteronormative ideals, while allowing reasonable public space and even celebration of difference so long as it's not *too* different. So long as the pretty young women writhing against each other in the straight club – and our pretty, white, upper-class academics – conform to our entrenched ideas about sexual desire and attractiveness – as long as they are obviously available for hetero-sex at any time, judged in part by their physical presentation, but also by the limited context within which their difference emerges – then they are welcomed into the public spaces allocated to heterosexual enactment and manifestation. In the ever-evolving realm of public discourse, deviance takes on a cloak of "respectability" in direct proportion to who is advocating it. The public performance of femininity certainly goes a long way to negating the connotations of deviant sexuality – much as an inelegant belch is made charming when delivered from the lips of an Angelina Jolie or a Julia Roberts, so is "arse-fuck" and femdom talk made charming when delivered from educated, young, lipsticked, upper-class mouths. Judith Butler[41] warns us that speech is constitutive of one's identity because it is "the reiterative and citational practice by which discourse produces the effects it names". Here Butler argues that the speech creates the act, and that speech therefore constitutes our identity – when the doctor remarks, "it's a girl", he creates the gender for the infant. But we would argue that this is not quite right. Though our identities are in many ways constituted through speech, it is only one reflection – an often inaccurate one – of the person we are. Thus we can point to someone and say "she is a deviant", but when the "she" in question physically belies the speech by looking decidedly straight and feminine, the speech act becomes confused and fails to perform. In other words, the lips may say one thing, but the performance of femininity says quite another. The label of deviant fails to stick in spite of the discourses employed in explanation – indeed, even performing the deviant acts themselves fails to create transgression for such women, if performed within the context of hegemonic femininity. One can almost picture straight men lining up to watch!

Heterosexuality itself is a non-category in this discourse, defining itself only in direct relation to what is deviant from it. Sedgwic argues that

> the silent uninterrogated nature of heterosexuality has come to mean that heterosexuality does not count as sexuality at all, to the point where it is in effect the opposite of sex. Therefore, to speak of non-normative sexuality is to transgress and stand outside of established law, ideology and discourse.[42]

Heterosexuals have no need of examining their sexuality simply because they only have a sexuality in direct proportion to whatever challenges there are to it. But we have argued that simply speaking of non-normative sexuality does not necessarily lead to transgression – indeed, the very performance of sometime deviant acts in certain contexts may be negated by those very contexts, be it hegemonic femininity in the academic arena, or the public space of the straight club, or the even broader public space of celebrity. Non-normative sexuality, we suggest, becomes transgressive in either (or both) speech and act only in the context of shame – that is, in the context within which the would-be transgressor has something at stake in coming out. What this means is that the moral geography of sexuality continues to be mapped out according to heteronormative ideals of romantic heterosexual love and sex, procreation, marriage and the family, marginalizing any real challenge to those ideals and securing any transgressive acts and identities in deviant subcultures so that they become visible only in the service of the mainstream. Meanwhile, public discourses continue to posture deviance while at the same time constraining it in ways that appear transgressive, but are, in reality, thoroughgoingly normative.

Part 3

8

OUT OF CONTEXT

The moral economy of sex and harm

Introduction

So far in this book we have argued that public discourses of sex, and what constitutes sexual harm, change over time and space. In Part 3, we engage with the ways in which we construct notions of harm, particularly "sex harm", according to the discourses that dominate a particular discipline or context. By arguing that a large proportion of what is considered sex harm is governed through the market, and that sex work, for example, may or may not be considered harmful according to which consumers it targets and which markets govern it, we differentiate between harm and "moral sensibilities", and examine the extent to which harm is contextual or intrinsic. We also suggest that theorists and the general public alike make a fatal mistake in attributing intrinsic harm to such activities as prostitution, adult entertainment and other forms of sexual commerce. We argue that it is not prostitution, or adult entertainment, or sex on the internet, that is harmful. Rather, it is pathological, systemic inequalities and entrenched disadvantage that are harmful, and that harm in these contexts is expressed in the way inequality and disadvantage are played out through sexual commerce and intimate relations.

By and large, the moral economy of sex is capitalistic – that is, governed by choice and supply–demand markets, except where the likelihood of harm provides a counterpoint. Because sex and sexual commerce are associated with harm and violence, the moral economy of sex is constrained by public health discourses about "harm minimization" and "harm reduction" that serve to regulate sex, including the enjoyment of sex and the commercial marketing of sex, that is outside the proper constraints of a heteronormative value system. Thus prostitution and "adult entertainment", for example, are activities that tend to be criminalized or at least highly regulated, firstly because they are often viewed in the context of violence and organized crime, and secondly because they challenge traditional structures such as the family, marriage and procreation. We will refer to activities such as prostitution and adult entertainment as "sexual commerce", bearing in mind that sex is the major issue.

Markets as the embodiment of sex

Sex plays a crucial role in the western economy; it dominates the marketplace more than any other commodity, and is a cornerstone of popular culture. Sex is used to market an enormous variety of consumer goods, from shoes and clothes to holidays and home furnishings. But sex has also become a commodity in its own right, and not just in the "alternative" economies of underground sex work, cybersex and pornography.

Secret Diary of a Call Girl, a television series based on the award-winning blog by Belle de Jour, recounts the experiences of a high-class sex worker. Belle is a twenty-something, university-educated woman whose love of "sex and meeting people",[1] combined with a series of bad experiences in job hunting, motivated her to choose a life as an "escort". Belle's tales of expensive underwear, luxury hotels and literary discussions suggest prostitution is an enviable career choice for young women – certainly better than "badly-paid temp work".[2] With comparisons to *Sex and the City*, *Bridget Jones*, "but with fisting"[3] and *Pretty Woman*, it is a romantic take on prostitution: "sex at The Ritz with Jude Law look-alikes, followed by dessert at *Harvey Nichols'* diamond counter".[4] Glamour, luxury and upmarket settings, it seems, make sex work palatable to the consumer of popular culture in a way that the over-made-up hooker hanging out on the corner of some seedy bar in Brixton never has.

Indeed, the up-market sex worker has risen to such monumental heights in popular culture that Belle (or rather, her alter ego, Brooke Magnanti) now writes an occasional column for *The Guardian*. Prostitution of the seedy, back-rooms-and-pimps variety may be considered immoral and illegal by the majority of the population, but if you don't actually have to stand face to face with it, it's not half-bad, apparently; in fact, it's rather sexy and *avante garde*. The appeal of a rags-to-riches story, of a girl who beats the odds, is always a welcome addition to the lore of the modern market economy – no matter that she had to have penetrative anal sex with numerous men she didn't know, risk disease and exploitation, and possible prosecution. The fact that she makes big money, that she is young, glamorous and educated, makes her the envy of the modern heterosexual woman and the object of desire of the modern heterosexual man.

With the success of the first *Call Girl* television series in the UK in 2007, two further series quickly followed, as did distribution worldwide to countries and regions as diverse as Canada, Israel, France, Poland, Turkey, the Middle East and Finland. In the USA, *Secret Diary of a Call Girl* premiered on the Showtime network, attracting the highest ratings the cable channel had seen in four years. However, even prior to the airing of its first episode, debate raged as to whether this "naughty new drama"[5] was a suitable portrayal of prostitution. Certainly, it is selective in its "rose-coloured view" of the sex industry.[6] Belle has an agent rather than an exploitative pimp,[7] for example, which brings notions of celebrity to the career choice, and the series is also conveniently free of drugs and violence. As Daubney[8] notes, "the series' grand conceit is that it glamorises the world's least glamorous industry".

These criticisms were countered by the suggestion that such experiences, though in the minority among sex workers, also need to be told. Playing on the "happy hooker" myth,[9] this popular media representation of prostitution combines soft porn and voyeurism in a romantic fantasy. It is clear that the reality of some sex work – downtrodden, diseased, damaged and drug-addicted prostitutes – does not make for good television viewing[10] – except perhaps on BBC World News. Indeed, a recent survey of stories about prostitution on the BBC website is instructive. Out of a total of over 100 stories accessed at the time of writing, most were concerned with the plight of illegal immigrant women forced into sex work because they had little or no other means of support. One story reported a couple in Ireland who had been charged with illegally importing foreign nationals for sex work. Another reported on a radio interview with the middle-class ex-prostitute author of a book on the subject, who had turned to sex work after getting into debt.

Still more stories revolve around the prominence and dire conditions of prostitution as a female occupation in non-western countries such as Pakistan. Such stories report the lurid facts about what sex work is like for a lot of women, so how can series such as *Call Girl* – and the book and blog on which it is based – become so popular, especially in light of the damning social science, public health and feminist discourses currently circulating on the subject?

In this section, we challenge the contradictions implicit in social constructions of sex, sexual commerce and bodies. On the one hand, dominant discourses about sex make it explicit that sex should be enjoyed within heteronormative institutions and structures. According to these discourses, sex outside these constraints causes harm, especially to women. Women are constructed as victims of aberrant sexual practices and values that do violence both to women's bodies and to their subjectivity. On the other hand, media discourses about sex, sexuality and titillation abound, encouraging both men and women to enjoy and exploit their sexuality, suggesting that sexuality should be subject to free choice and that sex is something that can and should be bought and sold because men want it and women embody it. There is no harm, according to this view, in using sex for commercial gain.[11]

An analysis of both sets of discourse suggests, however, that the role of sex in our society is much more complex, and littered with pockets of resistance that call into question our preconceived beliefs about sex and bodies, especially in the marketplace. The following examines the ways bodies are used in the governing of sex and gender, and the kinds of resistance that have arisen in response to that. In doing so, it unpacks the notion of "harm" and questions the automatic association of sex with power and knowledge on the one hand, and disenfranchisement and exploitation on the other.

The social construction of harm

"Harm" is a term that means to injure, but what constitutes injury depends on both the context within which the term is employed and who is being injured. One common example of the way in which we talk about sex harm comes to light when we look at discourses about women being harmed by sexual commerce; that is, discourses that describe either women in general being injured by the sex industry, or particular sex workers or strippers being victims of abuse simply because they are sex workers.

The first definition of harm condemns all sex work as injurious. The Coalition Against Trafficking in Women Australia (CATWA)[12] states on its website that "prostitution per se is a form of violence against women", that "prostitution, in itself, is intrinsically traumatising" and that "the harm is physical, social, emotional, and psychological". Moreover, "the harm extends to all women and humanity as a whole – socially, culturally, and globally".[13] Thus even women (and men, too, one can extrapolate) who are not involved in or exposed to prostitution are harmed by it.

How can it be said that someone who has never, and will never, come into contact with prostitution is harmed by it? CATWA states that in First World countries, prostitutes are disproportionately drawn from marginalized populations, creating a vicious cycle of drug and alcohol dependency. Developing countries are becoming reliant on "sex tourism to attract foreign currency", which again reinforces the domination of the strong over the weak.[14] This, in turn, reinforces attitudes toward, and subsequently stigmatizes, marginalized groups, and especially women, entrenching the kinds of discriminatory and divisive attitudes that lead to an unhealthy society. *Ipso facto*, prostitution is intrinsically harmful, regardless of where it is taking place and who is involved, because it contributes to the breakdown of society. This kind of harm we shall call "global harm" in recognition of the fact that individuals, groups and even nations need not be aware of being harmed, even though they may be subject to insidious damage imposed through the presence of prostitution. This kind of harm is similar to what Feinberg[15] terms "harm to public interests", that is, harm to something that most people in society would have an interest in – the elimination of poverty and violence, for example.[16] Feminist discourses most commonly express this view of prostitution.

The second kind of harm focuses on specific harms to individuals directly involved in prostitution, most commonly expressed in public health discourses about "harm minimization" or "harm reduction". The following passage expresses this view:

> Sex work is an extremely dangerous profession. The use of harm reduction principles can help to safeguard sex workers' lives in the same way that drug users have benefited from drug use harm reduction. Sex workers are exposed to serious harms: drug use, disease, violence, discrimination, debt, criminalisation, and exploitation. … Successful and promising harm reduction strategies are available: education, empowerment, prevention, care, occupational health and safety, decriminalisation of sex workers, and human rights based approaches.[17]

This harm reduction focuses on "pragmatic and evidence based health policies" that focus more on keeping sex workers safe than on eliminating or reducing sex work. Proponents of this view often argue that legalizing prostitution allows sex workers to "escape pimps and organised crime", allows more effective public health measures to be instituted, and removes sex work as a "victimless crime".[18] An associated concept is that of "risk", which focuses on discourses identifying individuals and groups as "at-risk" or "high-risk". Sex work is considered to be a high-risk activity for the individual sex worker as well as the client. In this sense, sex work is a victimless crime because the discourses assume that both parties have consented, that sex work is a valid – if risky – career choice, rather than an uncontrollable reaction to systemic marginalization and poverty. Sex work is therefore a simple commercial transaction between consenting parties and therefore should not be criminalized. The public health discourse argues that the threat of criminal conviction drives sex workers to the margins of society and therefore causes them to be at risk of harm.[19]

The debate on whether prostitution harms individuals or entire societies is discussed in chapter 9. The point of using this example here is to highlight the way in which notions of risk and harm are used in the governing of sex and bodies, and can lead to contradictory points of view concerning how those entities ought to be governed. This is further complicated by media discourses on sex and bodies, which tend to celebrate risk.

When risk is good

Sex sells, but that is not the only reason we engage with it in popular culture. We are, it seems, caught in a conundrum of trying to reconcile current discourses about the harm caused by sex with discourses about sexual empowerment and knowledge. The media depict sex as power, and celebrate sexualities and bodies in ways that are quite unique. The rise of television shows such as *Sex and the City* and *Secret Diary of a Call Girl*, as noted above, provide us with a voyeuristic insight into what sexual power might be like. Women in these shows use their sexual power, and that power is considered to be positive and self-affirming. They are not merely objects for male sexual satisfaction, and they provide a pedagogic framework within which young women may learn about sexual power. These women are taking risks, in terms of both the relationships and practices in which they engage, but the risk is seen as empowering. The woman who uses her body in sexually and commercially satisfying ways has confronted the risk of harm and overcome it – she is thus stronger for the experience. These positive affirmations of women's sexual experiences in the face of possible harm show us that women's desire is not secondary to men's, or necessarily vulnerable to exploitation. Rather, female desire affirms the positive space that women can occupy in the worlds of sex and commerce.

At the same time, however, we see women's bodies – women's sexual bodies – being used to sell all kinds of products, and being presented in ways that do not seem so self-affirming. Advertisements depicting heterosexual couples in sexual poses are used to sell many different products, but most specifically we see this genre being used in ads for designer jeans, alcohol and perfume. An informal survey of ads conducted by genderads.com also reports several clothing designers using sex to sell their wares. Clothing chain French Connection UK (which cutely and ubiquitously markets itself as FCUK) is one company that almost overuses sex in advertising. One supposes that, since the acronym already has us thinking in terms of sex, they might as well capitalize on it.

Whether these ads actually harm social perceptions of women or sex is another matter, however. Scott Lucas of genderads.com suggests that ads such as that for Lavazza coffee, which depicts a highly attractive, naked heterosexual couple engaging in sex play in a vat of coffee beans, makes fools of consumers. He also argues that using sex to sell products "ignores the fact that society is prone to sexual violence, rape and unwanted pregnancies", all of which are obvious harms,[20] and that many of these ads stereotype femininity and masculinity, a practice that objectifies both male and female bodies, thereby denying the subjectivity of the people depicted in the ads.

Sex harm as the subject of jurisprudential concern

Theorists such as Feinberg[21] have constructed in-depth legal analyses of the meaning of harm with respect to sex, appealing to essentialist principles that supposedly can be universalized across times and cultures. For Feinberg, harm is a set, quantifiable entity, and the amount of harm in any activity can be discovered and quantified. What constitutes harm depends on how much an activity impinges negatively on the interests of individuals without their consent, where what constitutes one's interests is very much subjective. Thus Feinberg argues that it is perfectly reasonable for an individual to claim that they are harmed by having to witness something they find morally and personally objectionable, and indeed for entire societies to do the same. He refers to such harms as "harms to the public sensibility".[22] Feinberg's meaning is best exemplified in his own hypothetical case study, from *The Moral Limits of the Criminal Law*,[23] which we considered in chapter 5, in which he proposes we consider being faced with a variety of potentially offensive behaviours while sitting on a bus. These behaviours range from having to sit opposite a passenger who hasn't bathed in a week, to one who continually scratches, drools, farts and belches, to one who is completely naked, and on to a variety of more and more "offensive" behaviours such as masturbation, sexual intercourse and sado-masochistic sex acts.[24]

The point of the exercise is to determine "whether there are any human experiences that are harmless in themselves, yet so unpleasant that we can rightly demand legal protection from them even at the cost of other persons' liberties".[25] He concludes that the fact that the average person would find these activities threatening and disgusting does indeed give us a right to protection from them. Indeed, one of the examples on the bus is that of two men kissing and fondling each other. Given the date of the book – 1985 – Feinberg might be forgiven for suggesting that the majority of men at least would find *that* threatening and therefore should not reasonably be expected to be exposed to it. While it is probably reasonable to assume most people would indeed be offended by being forced to witness public copulation or bondage/domination/sado-masochism (BDSM), for example, this very reasoning also underlies the kinds of discourse surrounding the stigmatization of public displays of a less shocking nature, for example, public displays of affection by same-sex couples. Even in the current climate of supposed toleration, it wouldn't be rash to suggest that many people would feel offended by having to witness such displays and, since the offence is so widespread, they are also correct in believing they have a right to be protected from it by law.

The natural corollary of this reasoning, however, is that the same people who might be titillated by reading about Belle de Jour's exploits into sexual commerce may be equally horrified if faced with bevies of sex workers in their neighbourhoods or near their places of employment. What doesn't harm the eyes or the sensibilities when witnessed on television or when read in a book suddenly becomes grossly offensive when witnessed in close proximity and in real time. The fact that Belle is educated, white, middle class and very attractive works in her favour, of course, but how many people would be happy knowing they lived across the street from a brothel – even a legal one? If it wasn't the thought of plummeting property values, certainly the thought of women selling their bodies several times a night and engaging in debaucherous acts would provide grounds for offence. It is not a huge jump to move from needing legal protection from the proximity of sexual commerce, to needing protection from the proximity of convicted paedophiles, or even homosexuals.

Markets as the embodiment of sex harm

Sex becomes more acceptable where it is marketable. This includes the selling of sex, which, while morally or medically questionable from some perspectives, as we have seen above, becomes acceptable when it is turned into a marketable commodity, as in when Belle de Jour made selling sex exotic and socially acceptable by blogging and writing about it. The issues here again are choice and consent – being an informed consumer is all that is needed to justify the consumption of sex in the marketplace. Sex is used to market goods and services because it is seen as something men want and women want to embody. Harm caused by sex that is outside the market is more often considered wrong; for example, rape, rape in marriage and sex with the underaged. However, where sex harm is sold as BDSM or in erotica, it becomes potentially exotic and acceptable. What this suggests is that it is not these activities *per se* that are harmful, but the context in which they are carried out.

It is not the fact that a Pakistani woman sells her body for sex that causes her harm; it is the fact that her economic and social circumstances are such that she has no other choice but to enter into unsafe sexual commerce, putting herself at great risk of harm. Julia Roberts sells her body in *Pretty Woman* because she ran away from home as a teenager and this is the only way she, as an unskilled woman, can make ends meet. Should we stop to question what social structures and institutions make it necessary for a young woman to tear herself away from home and family in the first place? Should we perhaps be challenging the assumption that teens must live up to the stereotypical, achievement-oriented lifestyle of the heteronormative ideal – do well at school, study, get involved in sports and other activities, be "well-rounded", attractive and slim? There is nowhere for teens to go who do not fit this predetermined mould; even government and academic research into "at-risk" teens labels them if they don't conform. They have no other choice but to break away from an institutional structure for which they are a poor fit. Roberts's character's choice of sex work as a career is seen as problematic only because she is poor and disempowered. But the cause of her poverty and disempowerment are not directly related to the fact that she is a prostitute; rather, she is doomed to disempowerment and exploitation as a sex worker because she is forced to sell herself on street corners to the highest bidder – something at which Belle de Jour would certainly cringe. It is lack of employable skills, ready cash and social support that create the harm for Roberts's character, not the fact that she engages in sex work.

This is perhaps best illustrated by Belle's own words, in responding to the supposed moral outrage often expressed toward people in her profession. After her first experience of sex work, she goes home to bed, as usual.

> The next morning I woke up in my own bed. Held my hand up, stared at it for ages. Was something supposed to be different? Should I have felt victimized, abused? I couldn't say. The finer points of feminist theory didn't seem to apply. Things felt as they always had. Same hand, same girl. I got up and made breakfast.[26]

The feminist critic might argue that, regardless of whether she felt harmed, Belle was indeed injured by her experience – she just didn't know it. This kind of harm, which is grounded in ideas of "false consciousness", are common in both the feminist and conservative literature against sexual commerce. This literature is examined in some detail in chapter 9. For the purposes of this chapter, it is necessary merely to highlight the main point of the argument: that it is not the fact that a woman sells her body, or parades around in front of men for money, or strips for them in public for money, that causes her harm; it is the fact that women are being used by men – are being exploited by men – that causes them harm. This view is grounded in the idea that women might be victims of sexual exploitation against their will – that they are, in fact, "cultural dupes",[27] incapable of understanding that what they are doing, or what is happening to them, is harmful to them.[28] We suggest this view is not only insulting to women, but completely inaccurate.

Young women in general have become the recent target of second-wave feminists of the 1980s and 1990s for their willingness to engage in what has been described as "ladette" behaviour; that is, for being willing to act much the same as young men do by engaging in drinking, smoking, swearing and casual sex. Feminists such as Ariel Levy denounce these young women for their attitudes and behaviours, and for wearing provocative clothes, as a sign of "faux empowerment".[29] She claims that such behaviours serve only to continue the objectification of women, not only by men, but by women as well – women who, in the wake of the freedoms achieved by those second-wave feminists – ought to know better. But younger feminists disagree, and loudly it seems, claiming that such criticisms are merely one more way of trying to control their behaviour. Nina Funnell, for example, argues that feminists "ought to engage with such narratives rather than dismissing them" as simple cultural dupes.[30]

> A number of my friends take pole-dancing classes. Another two have had boob jobs. And many of my friends enjoy big nights out on the booze. They also

swear, smoke and have sex. Yet these women are highly successful, motivated, intelligent individuals. They would take offence at the suggestion they have been coerced or duped into a life of ladette hedonism.[31]

Similarly, Catharine Lumby argues that young girls and women who engage with fashion and popular culture are able to remain participatory and critical subjects of both.[32] Interestingly, however, Lumby also challenges the idea that older British women who travel to the Dominican Republic to engage in social and sexual encounters with young men half their age are simply acting as sexual tourists – much as men do. She claims that these women, coming as they are from positions of vulnerability (a result, she claims, of growing up in a society in which they were treated as sexual currency), are themselves exploited, just as they are exploiting the young men they meet.[33] But this seems contradictory – to allow subjectivity to younger, but not to older women, based on their respective histories, is to deny the real freedoms women have claimed over the past few decades, freedoms that ought not be policed by feminists any more than they ought to be policed by social attitudes or the criminal justice system. Instead, perhaps, as Funnell argues, "it would be more fruitful to try to understand the cultural significance and reasons behind" such behaviour.

Conclusion

This chapter has provided an overview of the notion of harm, specifically sexual harm, and opened up for discussion how we think about the harms often thought to be inherent in sex crimes such as prostitution. Chapters 9 and 10 extrapolate from these musings, with a particular focus on unpacking discourses surrounding sexual commerce (chapter 9) and sex trafficking (chapter 10). The fact that these two are often conflated, both in the academic literature and in media discourses, provides an interesting starting point for this section. With this in mind, chapter 9 explores the sexual economy, its boundaries and alleged harms, and how it is governed, while chapter 10 examines the impact of sex trafficking on public perceptions and treatment of immigration and immigrants, particularly with respect to women.

9

SEXUAL COMMERCE

Introduction

The Eros Guide[1] is an online adult entertainment guide that offers advertising for independently employed erotic entertainers. Established twelve years ago, the site makes its money by creating and posting advertisements for local escorts, fetish specialists and erotic masseurs for a fee, depending on the size of photos, video capabilities and other extras. By answering some simple questions about gender, location and the entertainment being sought, the site can direct individuals to a range of services, other sites or advertisements, which include male and female escorts, adult toys, live webcams and adult dating. The Eros Guide claims to be the largest listing of erotic entertainers in the world, and includes contact information for massage, erotic art, strippers, nightlife, shopping, erotica, club listings and events in any local area. Interestingly, given our previous discussion about the moral panic surrounding sex with children, this site has also voluntarily registered with parental controls such as Net Nanny, Cyber Patrol, Cybersitter and Safe Surf, "to keep your children safe from adult materials". Based on research from other sites, peak times for hits are generally between 12:30 and 1:00 in the afternoon, and 5:30 and 5:36 in the evening. A clear moral code of no full frontal nudity is in place, especially given the time of day when most visits to the site occur. As the owner of one site maintains, "Doing it this way gives people more access to our site from offices ... we don't want them to get sued for sexual harassment if they have our website on their computer screen."[2]

According to Edelman,[3] 36 per cent of internet users visit at least one adult website each month, with an average visit lasting 11.6 minutes. While traffic to online adult entertainment sites is less concentrated than retail sites (where the top 500 adult entertainment sites account for 56 per cent of adult site traffic, compared with the top 500 retail sites, which account for 76 per cent of all retail site traffic), the adult entertainment trade's AVN Media Network reported that US online adult entertainment in 2006 reached $2.6 billion of revenue, a 13 per cent increase from 2005. Moreover, such expenditure now exceeds spending at adult clubs.

There is no doubt that, over the past thirty years, the demand for commercially available sexual services has massively increased and diversified along technological, spatial and social lines. Leaving aside the pornographic part of the sex industry, which we have discussed in detail in chapter 4, sexual commerce now encompasses live sex shows, fetish clubs, adult entertainment clubs, escort agencies, telephone and cybersex contacts, drive-through striptease venues and organized sex tours of developing countries. Sexual commerce has become a "large, complex, multi-billion-dollar industry", producing and supporting a global economy in sectors as diverse as tourist resorts and hotel chains, mobile telephone companies, paid television networks and information technology.[4]

This chapter examines the ways in which harm is understood to be an integral part of these encounters precisely because they involve sex in exchange for money. This dominant discourse, begun with the rise of first-wave feminism in the nineteenth century, instigated legislative and policy changes around the harm of prostitution. Those same arguments drive encounters with sexual commerce today. However, of what relevance are laws about the public nuisance of prostitution, for example, when the industry is largely indoors and online? Similarly, how useful are arguments about the inherent exploitation of sexual commerce, when many non-commercial sexual relations are perceived as recreational or leisure pursuits, rather than emotionally meaningful sexual encounters? This chapter explores these issues in detail and offers some insights into the changing nature of both sexual commerce and sexual relations more generally in the twenty-first century. To do so, it engages with the relationship between harm, sexual commerce, society and the law, as well as positioning these changes over space and time.

Markets as sex harm

Current understandings of sexual commerce as harmful have their roots in the mid-nineteenth century in England and Europe, when the idea that prostitution was a dangerous form of sexual activity became part of a new social attitude to sex. As we have noted in previous chapters, pornography, homosexuality and incest were also being identified, named and regulated at this time. Sexual activity outside the conjugal relation was being positioned as immoral, harmful and unnatural, and women who sold sex were one of the groups targeted for attention.

Historical understandings of harm

From the mid-nineteenth century, a whole raft of changes were occurring simultaneously, which came together in social concern over the prostitute. As noted in previous chapters, there was a new way of thinking about the relationship between children and sex, and the role of the family in protecting children from sex. Marriage and the domestic sphere became the gateway to respectability and stability. "It testified to moral and financial respectability; it secured the legitimacy of children; it offered cheap and safer pleasures than the outside world and it was a source of virtues and emotions that could be found nowhere else."[5] In this new family model, women were given the role of dependent domestic virtue, offering love, nurture and support as well as appropriate moral guidance and conjugal relations. This increasing idealization of domesticity required a capacity to censure extra-marital sex, and this was done through the continued extension of the criminal law, which became focused on prostitution as unrespectable, illicit and immoral. "The paradox was, that the more ideology stressed the role of sex within conjugality, the more it was necessary to describe and regulate those forms of sexuality which were outside of it".[6]

The prostitute flouted Victorian ideals of respectable femininity by being both sexually available and sexually experienced as well as economically independent. She was also a member of the "dangerous classes", the casual labouring poor who inhabited a social underworld which was the focus of "deep-seated social fears and insecurities, most vividly expressed in the images of filth and contagion associated with the 'Great Unwashed'".[7] Finally, the prostitute was seen as the conduit of infection to respectable society, either because of her "seduction by degenerate aristocrats" or the constant temptation she offered to middle-class sons "who could not pass along the street in the evening without meeting and being accosted by women of the town at every step".[8]

In the mid-nineteenth century, these concerns over prostitution came together in the establishment of the *Contagious Diseases Acts* in England, with similar measures to control prostitution enacted in European countries and their colonies.[9] Very briefly, the *Contagious Diseases Acts* were passed in an attempt to control sexually transmitted disease in the armed forces, and they were initiated in 1864, 1866 and 1869 in eleven, thirteen and then eighteen garrison ports and towns in England and Ireland. The original Act provided that a woman identified as a prostitute by a plainclothes member of the metropolitan police was to undergo an examination and, if found diseased, she could be detained in a hospital for up to three months. The new clauses of 1866 "established a system of compulsory periodic fortnightly inspection or examination of all known prostitutes under a well organized system of medical police".[10] Discovery of disease meant internment in a lock-up hospital for a period not exceeding six months, although in 1869 this was increased to nine months. In Australia, similar laws were passed. Queensland and Tasmania enacted such laws in 1868 and 1879, respectively, although the Queensland laws went further than either England or Tasmania, and applied to civilian populations as opposed to simply garrison towns. In France, a state system to control prostitution was established after 1828 through a series of administrative decisions enacted by the Parisian police, who imposed both state regulation and mandatory medical examinations on prostitutes. Such ideas were emulated across Europe.[11]

Given that the clients of prostitutes were never tested for disease, the purpose of the Acts was rendered totally nugatory. However, fused within this Act was the reinforcement of a double standard of sexual morality which justified male sexual access to a class of fallen women, and penalized women for engaging in the same vice as men. Therefore it was not surprising that those opposed to the Acts included a loose alliance of middle-class non-conformists, feminists and radical working men, who challenged the Acts as both immoral and unconstitutional.[12] The Acts were immoral because they officially sanctioned male vice and the double standard of sexual morality, and unconstitutional because they subjected women to a degrading internal examination by male doctors and used police to enforce sexual and social discipline among the poor.

It was partly in reaction to these Acts that the "image of the prostitute as vile and disgusting" was replaced by the prostitute as a victim, "an ordinary working class woman who needed rescuing".[13] Certainly, some famous moral reformers of the time, such as William Acton in England and Parent-Duchâtelet in Paris, had already suggested that prostitution was a transitory occupation, and that prostitutes were nothing more than victims of poverty.[14] Such a way of thinking about prostitutes was carried further by those who agitated against the *Contagious Diseases Acts* and called for their repeal. The prostitute became a symbol of sexual and economic exploitation under industrial capitalism, the result of seduction by "aristocratic libertines". Such accounts depicted the prostitute as an innocent victim of male lust, social injustice and exploitation. It is these contradictory themes of exploitation and victimization, and seduction, promiscuity and disease, that have remained central to current concerns over the harm of sexual commerce.

Modern understandings of harm

That the global sex industry is growing and its forms proliferating is now a conventional wisdom. According to Agustin,[15] to depict the modern sex industry accurately, "all commercial goods and services of an erotic and sexual kind must be included". This would necessarily widen the gaze beyond prostitution to erotic phone lines, escort services, films and videos, souvenirs, toys, clothes, equipment, and live and virtual performances via web cameras. Sites are similarly expanded to take into account bars, restaurants, cabarets, clubs, brothels, discotheques, saunas, massage parlours, sex shops with private booths, hotels, flats, internet sites, cinemas and anywhere else that sex is offered for sale on an occasional basis, including stag and hen nights, shipboard festivities and modelling parties. Finally, the actors involved would multiply beyond direct buyers and sellers of sex to business owners and investors, non-sexual employees (waiters, cashiers, guards, drivers, accountants, lawyers, doctors), and middlemen and women who facilitate business processes (travel agents, travel guides, estate agents, newspaper and magazine editors, internet entrepreneurs). However, our reactions to commercial sex – moral revulsion "and/or resigned tolerance" – have little changed over the past 150 years, and as a consequence the identified harms have also remained the same.

First, by promoting adultery and promiscuity, the sex industry challenges the sanctity of the family and monogamous intimate relations between husbands and wives. Within such a conceptualization of harm, the exchange of money is largely irrelevant, although it may be seen to encourage the seller and admonish the guilt of the buyer, and thus to enable promiscuity and adultery. Access to commercial sex is positioned at the forefront of marriage and family breakdowns by increasing the capacity for cheating and infidelity. This harm speaks to an idealized form of intimate sexual relations, a quest for the return to traditional relations between sex, romantic love and family. "The act of making love with a woman is I believe something that is best encountered when one is deeply in love and has a connection with that person."[16] As the idea of non-commercial sexual relations outside marriage has become more acceptable, the harm of the sex industry has shifted from that of promiscuity and adultery to the harm of impersonal and unemotional sexual acts. Commercial sex becomes the exemplar of a society in which traditional values associated with sex are debased and commercialized.

The second harm, and that which has most salience in contemporary society, is the harm of commercial sex to women. Here, the capacity of the buyer (usually a man) to purchase sexual access to the seller (usually a woman) exemplifies the inherent inequality of both gender relations and the class structure. This harm is intrinsic to sexual commerce and is due to the exchange itself, which exemplifies the exploitation and victimization of all women. This is because the sex industry commodifies and objectifies women as sex objects for male pleasure. The commercial transaction exemplifies the unequal power relations between men and women in society, since the capacity to purchase gives ownership over property. In this way of thinking, men purchase women's bodies for their own sexual gratification. Central to this harm is the assertion that there is an intrinsic property of sex that makes its commodification wrong. As a consequence, women involved in sexual entertainment are oppressed by a system that privileges male pleasure over female pleasure and safety. Such a transaction objectifies women's bodies for men, who use them as commodities for pleasure. These oppressed women are thus victims of a system that forces them to commodify very private, intimate sexual behaviours, and therefore sexually objectify themselves in their involvement in the industry.[17]

Because of this harm, the sex industry subordinates, degrades and victimizes all women by offering a group of women to be available to sexually service men. In fact, the sex industry represents women as sexual servants to men, as they are a class of women who exist to service men's sexual needs. This contributes directly to the inferiority of women in society because it helps to shape notions of female subordination. Commercial sex becomes one of the more extreme examples of harm in a patriarchal society, where women have little or no access to power, and great earning potential through the use of their sexualized bodies. Finally, the sex industry is positioned as violence against women, akin to rape and sexual abuse. Violence is intrinsic and endemic to the sex industry. In this way of thinking, as we saw in chapter 8, commercial sex is not wrong because it causes harm, rather it constitutes a harm in and of itself. Any distinction between forced and voluntary prostitution, for example, is a myth, since coercion is always involved, even if the worker is unaware of it. Moreover, differentiating street prostitution from escort work or sex trafficking is illusory, since the simple act of purchase or money exchange is the harm.[18]

There is, of course, a growing critique of such findings, especially in methodological terms, with research supporting a more nuanced understanding of the range of activities now included within sexual commerce. However, many of these statements about the harm of prostitution for women are philosophical and theoretical, rather than empirical, and speak to a more idealistic notion of sexual intimacy. The changing nature of this relationship in the context of the twenty-first century is discussed in more detail later in this chapter.

The third and final harm is to society more generally. Here, the sex industry is perceived to be integral to the perpetuation of organized crime, especially drug and people trafficking, the spread of sexually transmitted diseases, and an increase in sexual violence. Research does support some of these claims, especially with regard to prostitution. Relationships have been discovered across the world between the initial motivation to enter the industry and sex abuse as children or drug use as adults. Similarly, sexual abuse by clients, and exploitation by police, pimps and managers, has been found to be part of the life of some prostitutes, and evidence of coerced entry into prostitution via trafficking and organized crime has also been found. Finally, there is a pervasive fear of infection from prostitutes, in both a physical and a moral sense.[19]

However, there are variations dependent on the type of sex work. As Vanwe-senbeeck[20] notes, the results of HIV prevalence studies in North America and Europe show that those infected with HIV are primarily drug-using prostitutes. Similarly, those who enter prostitution due to a history of sexual victimization are generally young homeless women. Sexual victimization and exploitation is also related to the type of sex work performed, with indoor sex workers reporting much lower levels than street prostitutes, the latter being more vulnerable to legal intervention and police arrest as well as the experiences of violence.[21] Most importantly, most research on the harm of commercial sex continues to focus on the most vulnerable groups in the industry – predominantly street prostitutes and those in prison – and those with the additional problems of economic hardship, histories of sexual victimization, homelessness and drug addictions. These are then presented as features of sex work *per se*, and sexual commerce retains its relationship with misery, harm and victimization. And, while a relationship between sex work, organized crime and trafficking can be seen to exist, media claims that it has intensified over the past decade are virtually impossible to state with certainty. Rather, while sex work across national boundaries has always existed, it may be that certain patterns of migration have changed (from the non-western to the western world) or become more visible, "resulting in an exaggeration of its increasing magnitude worldwide".[22]

The harm of sexual commerce in the twenty-first century is remarkably similar to the harm of prostitution in the nineteenth century. This is because the relationship between sex, privacy and intimacy has remained virtually unchallenged during this time, despite shifts in sexual freedom and equality.

Rethinking the harm of sexual commerce

There is agreement that the sex industry is experiencing unparalleled growth at the beginning of the twenty-first century. This includes the increasing acceptability of strip clubs and lap-dancing bars, as well as sexual commercialization via the internet and mobile phones. The fact that the vast majority of sexual commerce occurs indoors may, of course, be a reaction to the zero-tolerance policies directed toward street prostitution, but it is also due to a changing shift in social relationships, structures and attitudes – a creation, if you like, of new moral communities.

Temporality and harm

Before the late eighteenth century, commercial sex was treated as one of an array of offences to be managed, without any special moralism. In the tenth century, for example, those to be banished for their crimes included "wizards, sorcerers, perjurers, conspirators to murder and horewenan, which included whores, fornicators and adulterers".[23] By the twelfth century, women who sold sex were positioned as a "necessary evil" that needed to be contained. By the middle ages, selling sex was an "integral part of urban life" and was not isolated as a particular problem. "In the pre-modern world picture, every object and being was believed to occupy its proper place for a reason, and large scale attempts to change fate did not make sense."[24] Similarly, in the seventeenth and eighteenth centuries, sexual misconduct was a serious matter, "but there was no reason to single it out as the ultimate wickedness".[25]

The issue here is that prostitutes did not have a distinguishable identity. Although laws were passed to regulate whoredom, the category "whore" was never defined. Rather, whoring referred to sexual relations outside marriage and connoted immorality or promiscuity. The issue of money was largely irrelevant, since the emphasis was on the behaviour, not the personal identity. The establishment in England of the *Vagrancy Act* of 1822 is a case in point. While the Act named prostitutes for the first time as one among other stigmatized groups who could be arrested, locating offenders was frustrated by the impossibility of agreeing on a definition. Those classified as prostitutes often included vagrants, professional beggars, cheats and thieves, as well as "any woman who yields to her passions and loses her virtue".[26]

Thus, in the nineteenth century, prostitution was still relatively unorganized. There were full-time vocational prostitutes, but there were also itinerant, casual, expedient and part-time prostitutes who used prostitution to supplement their income. The testimony of wives seeking divorce in Australia demonstrates the inadequacy of respectable solutions open to deserted wives and mothers, where earnings from domestic service, bar work or home dressmaking often had to be supplemented by friends and family, or by prostitution. At this time, there were no unemployment benefits for single women and the unemployment of married women was not recognized.[27] Prostitution also enabled married women to earn enough money to leave violent or drunken husbands, or to supplement an inadequate housekeeping allowance, especially given that the wages of unskilled workers at that time were not enough to support a family. Prostitution was also an obvious resort for women when cohabitation ceased. What is certainly clear is that women who worked as casual prostitutes did not see such activities as excluding them from "respectable" society. Prostitution was often a temporary income choice and did not affect their future plans for marriage.

The unorganized nature of prostitution and the unclear boundaries between casual and commercial sex were demonstrated through the venues utlilized. In Australia, brothels and hotels were used, but because of the mild weather, parks, paddocks, gardens, under bridges, behind buildings and railway stations, and alleyways also offered opportunities for clandestine affairs and part-time prostitution, which many women engaged in serially or simultaneously.[28] This demonstrates that the distinction between prostitution and other forms of casual sex and/or adultery were not clear cut. Divorced women could turn to casual prostitution to support themselves and their families before remarrying when their divorce was final. Others might work as a barmaid, cohabit with one man, and occasionally go home with one of her customers. According to Golder and Allen, these women had an essentially unsentimental attitude to their own bodies and sexuality, and did not make a rigid distinction between recreational and commercial sex.[29]

It could be argued that such a way of thinking about sex and commerce, especially an increasingly unsentimental attitude to bodies and sex, is occurring again. According to Attwood,[30] the rise of subscription internet pornography sites such as *Nerve* (established in 1997) and *SuicideGirls* (established in 2001) demonstrates how commerce is increasingly part of a way in which modern sexual identities and communities are produced. Following in the wake of more mainstream internet communities such as *Facebook*, *Myspace* and *YouTube,* sexually explicit representations online have developed which are as much about communication, participation, community and networks as they are about the distribution of commercial pornography. On *Nerve*, for example, a subscription fee of $7.00 per month gives members access to essays, poetry, fiction, advice, blogs, photography and personals as well as a premium photo gallery. On *SuicideGirls*, $12.00 per month gives members access to picture sites, videos, journals and blogs of the "Suicide Girls" as well as chat rooms, message boards and webcams. On such sites, access is related simultaneously to commerce and to community – "the more you pay, the more you belong".[31]

Interestingly, the models on *SuicideGirls* are more likely to be "purple-haired, pale and pierced" than "big-haired, big-breasted blondes". Moreover the focus on women's flesh and men's ejaculation is missing from these sites, which combine photographs of women in arty styles combined with coverage of music, news, art and culture, so that "sex is placed in a much broader cultural context" enabling porn to "take its place alongside other forms of culture and subculture".[32] Such "alt porn sites", like their more mainstream counterparts, blur the boundaries between producer and consumer, offering a "grassroots approach to sexuality".[33] They also connect with new forms of sex and sexuality, especially for women, popularized by TV shows such as *Sex and the City,* which bought into new models of hedonistic sexuality and recast sex and sexual interest as "literate and cool".[34]

Whether such sites demonstrate a clear shift in the relationship between sexual morality, intimacy and sexual commerce on a social scale equivalent to the shifts that occurred in the late nineteenth century is not clear. Certainly, there have been times in the twentieth century, especially during the 1930s and later in the 1960s, when attitudes to sex and bodies shifted drastically in certain subcultures, especially among the young. However, when teenage girls in Hong Kong and Japan can talk about "compensated dating" to refer to their practice of taking money for a date which will end in sex,[35] and when oral sex is discussed as the "new kiss"[36] by American teenagers, a shift of some kind is under way.

Space and harm

The appropriate relation between sex and the private sphere has a recent history, related to the rise of modern notions of privacy. In pre-modern times, it was considered socially acceptable to share a bed at an inn with a total stranger of either sex. Similarly, public and intergenerational nakedness was not seen as immoral or, necessarily, associated with sexual desire. In the same way, urinating and defecating in public space were permitted.[37] Given that sex was not given a different priority in the public psyche, sex in public was no more problematic. The rise of the domestic sphere, previously discussed, relegated all such bodily functions to clearly designated areas: the home, public toilets and brothels.

The criminalization of public sex began in the late nineteenth and early twentieth centuries, when for the first time soliciting became an offence in England and Australia. Prior to this time, prostitutes could be arrested only for behaving in a "riotous or indecent manner in public", or for being found "without sufficient visible lawful means of support".[38] In the twentieth and the twenty-first centuries, it is the public face of prostitution that bears the brunt of criminal justice interventions into the sex industry in all modern western democracies. In England, Canada, France, Italy and Finland, the public elements of soliciting are the most criminalized of all the illegal activities associated with prostitution. In Australia, although prostitution is legalized, this includes only the sale and purchase of sex in the private sphere, while restrictions on public prostitution are increased and street prostitutes are dealt with even more harshly than in a wholly criminalized system. When decriminalization is the regulatory option, as is the case in New Zealand and the Netherlands, public order is maintained through the provision of safe streets, where prostitutes can solicit and service their clients. These tend to be in industrial areas, away from schools, churches and the community at large.[39]

However, street prostitution is the smallest part of the prostitution industry, with estimates that it comprises less than 5 per cent of all prostitution-related activities,[40] and this does not include the vast array of other activities included in sexual commerce more generally. In such a situation, two issues emerge: first, a continued focus on policing the public spectacle of sex, and second, the invisibility of a large proportion of the sex industry.

According to Sanders,[41] the new commercial indoor sex environment involves the more traditional massage parlours, legal and illegal brothels, escort agencies and licensed saunas, as well as new erotic sites such as the Eros Guide, discussed at the beginning of this chapter, and which provide not only social networks, but also access to and facilitation of sexual services. Such community sex sites enable sellers, buyers and organizers to congregate through message boards and chat rooms in order to match people with similar interests.[42] Such websites also provide for feedback by purchasers (which can include recommendations to fellow purchasers), as well as announcement boards where women can advertise recent changes to their services. Interestingly, such websites often work within strict moral codes against the employment and purchase of sex with underage sex workers. Similarly, message boards tend to operate within a strict set of rules that determine what topics are acceptable, rejecting derogatory talk about sex workers or distasteful sexual activities. "Board moderators quickly delete messages that are inflammatory, and it has been known for contributors to be banned from the board for not sticking to the rules".[43]

According to Bernstein,[44] indoor sex workers were among the first to benefit from global internet technologies. It became "easier to work without third party management, to conduct business with minimal interference from the criminal justice system, and to reap greater profits by honing one's sales pitch to a more elite and specialised audience". The cost of web-based advertising is much less than other media, and the visual capacities of the web mean that various photo galleries can be included as well as more textual descriptions than in normal ads. "As a consequence, charges are normally considerably higher, possibly buying into the heightened expectation and desire associated with this form of visual communication".[45] Moreover, by advertising through speciality websites, sex workers can pitch their ads toward clients who are interested in their specific physical characteristics or the precise services they are willing to offer.

The internet can also provide a space for sex workers to pass on information, support and details relating to their own working practices. For example, a group of independent escorts have created an internet-based resource, "Support and Advice for Escorts" (www.saafe.info), which provides information to colleagues. The website includes extensive tips and case studies on topics as diverse as paying tax, ways of working and difficult clients, "offering a shortcut to the learning process in a business where experience really does count".[46]

Certainly, the internet has pushed contemporary culture to new frontiers of sexual tolerance "by eliminating the biggest obstacle to sexual services: shame and ignorance".[47]

> The ease and efficiency of these new technologies enabled online sexual commerce to shift the boundaries of social space, blurring the differences between underworld figures and respectable citizens ... strippers diversifying their assets and morphing into business-savvy internet artists, porn actors transforming into full time producers/distributors, ... and respectable companies and professionals who with the help of insider high-tech specialists, are discreetly establishing their own websites, both for pleasure and profit.[48]

Thus the rise of the internet has attracted new classes of individuals to participate in commercial transactions, as consumers and workers as well as producers and distributors. Partly as the result of economic restructuring and global recessions, individuals who are primarily white, native-born and relatively class privileged have found their way into sex work. If sexual labour is regarded as at best an unfortunate but understandable choice for women with few real alternatives, how are we to explain its increasing appeal to individuals with racial, class and educational advantages? The answer may lie in the reconfiguration of intimacy, sex and emotion in the twenty-first century.

Morality and harm

The decades between 1960 and 1980 in modern western democracies were characterized by the legalization of once illegal or stigmatized sexual behaviour, including increased access to contraception, abortion and divorce, the legalization of homosexuality and a relaxation of the censorship of pornography. Such a change demonstrated an acceptance of the need to adjust levels of sexual morality in the post-war context. What did not change was the appropriate relationship between sex and privacy. "The proper place for the exercise of sexual freedom was behind closed doors, safely encased within the private and domestic sphere. Conversely, the experience of sexual pleasure and the expression of sexuality in public continued to be stigmatised and marginalised as morally corrupt and obscene."[49]

However, according to Hawkes,[50] in the last two decades of the twentieth century, the distinctions between sex in the private sphere and sex in the public sphere were dissolving. Anonymous sexual encounters, once the defining feature of commercial sex, began to be offered as entertainment and leisure. The rise of reality TV, in the form of *Big Brother* and *Temptation Island*, "is a good example of the ways in which viewers were offered the position of voyeur to the sexual exhibitionism of the contestants". At the same time, the exponential rise in availability of pornographic material via sites such as *YouPorn* expanded via globalized internet technology.

Such "commodified eroticism" condones sex disengaged from any commitment or emotional ties. While such sexual encounters have traditionally been associated with prostitution, the twenty-first century seems to be offering sex without the stigma, due in part to increasing access to technology, but also to a shift in social organization and the resultant change in intimacy that have occurred over the past thirty years. These include a shift from a production- to a consumption-based economy, an increasing standard of living, and the rise of global information via internet communication technology, accompanied by a decline in marriage rates, a doubling of divorce rates, a 60 per cent increase in single-person households, and families populated by individuals spending only short periods of quality time together. According to Bernstein,[51] such changes have been responsible for the creation of a new erotic disposition, one that the market is well placed to satisfy.

More specifically, these changes indicate a shift in models of sexuality over the past 200 years: from a procreative orientation in pre-industrial society, to a companionate or relational model under industrial capitalism, to a recreational sexual ethic in our service-oriented, global information economy.[52] It is this most recent shift that has usurped the modern taboos surrounding sex, because it is "sex without commitment, transitory, anonymous and promiscuous".[53] Instead of being premised on marital or even durable relationships, the recreational sexual ethic derives its primary meaning from physical sensation. The message is that sex is a form of pleasure and there is nothing morally objectionable in acknowledging this fact. What is different is that this message is promulgated in the public sphere through advertising and the print and electronic media, and aimed as much at woman as at men – consider the success of *Sex and the City*. While the more traditional models of sex and sexuality derived their meaning "precisely from an ideological opposition to the marketplace" – based on intimate relations and domestically situated in the domestic private sphere – "recreational sexuality bears no antagonism to the sphere of public commerce".[54]

It also bears no antagonism to the relation between sex and fun. Historically, there has always been an association between sex and humour: think of Chaucer, Shakespeare, Congreve and Sheridan.[55] It was only from the nineteenth century that sex became associated with scientific and medical experts, and a much more serious business. In the late-twentieth century, that relation, too, seems to be diminishing, as sexual entertainment, sex tourism and sex holidays dissolve the distinction not only between public and private sex, but also between sex and commitment. According to Hawkes,[56] sex in the media is disengaged from relationships and emotions. "Sex is a commodity to be sold and consumed as a marker of self expression". In such an environment, the desire for sex is ever-present, of no more importance than the desire for food. Similarly, "vacation sex provides a context within which sex has no more moral content than windsurfing or scuba diving".[57]

In such a context of non-commercial sexual activity, buying and selling sex certainly becomes more mainstream. Bernstein[58] found that many of the middle-class, professional clients in her research desired a genuine emotionally intimate encounter, more real and human than satisfying oneself alone, yet they also desired a clear and bounded exchange. While this may seem contradictory or antagonistic, this is precisely the point. By actively removing themselves from the sex–romance nexus of the privatized nuclear family, "bounded authenticity" is compatible with their individually oriented daily life. Paid sex is not a sad substitute for something that ideally could be obtained in a non-commercial romantic relationship. Rather, it is an example of the ways in which a reorganization of social life, noted above, is reflected in shifts in personal lives and relationships. For some men, especially white, upper-middle-class professionals, living alone, having close emotional relationships with friends and paying for sex enables them to maintain their personal life on their own terms.

> Right now, I know a woman; she's pretty nice, but if I make love to her, she'll want a relationship. But I'm really used to living by myself. I go and come when I want, clean when I want. I love women, enjoy them; they feel comfortable around me … but I don't usually take the next step.[59]

For men already in a committed domestic relationship, commercial sex is positioned as the moral and emotional preference to an affair precisely because of the "clarifying effect of payment". In fact, in such a context, the non-commercial affair was more exploitative and dishonest than the clean cash-for-sex transaction. Other married men likened their desire for paid sex to consumer choice, "two hours of illicit fun", or "a nice change of pace".[60] In such a way of thinking, sexual expression bears no necessary connection to an intimate relationship, and a diversity of sexual partners and experiences is not sub-stitutive of an intimate relationship, but desirable in its own right. In such a context, "romantic love might sometimes be subordinated to, and judged unfavourably with, the more neutral, more cleanly exchangeable pleasures of eroticism".[61]

Conclusion

What is the harm of sexual commerce? There is no doubt that this industry involves risk, danger, exploitation, stigmatization. This chapter has not focused on these ele-ments, for two reasons. First, because the vast majority of research and theorizing, on prostitution in particular, discusses the industry in terms of harm. There are many more qualified than us to speak on this matter. Second, however, is that the notion of harm overwhelms understanding of the industry and it is difficult to find other ways of thinking about sexual commerce, the sex industry, prostitution. While the debate about the level of harm inherent in the sex industry is ongoing, this chapter has sought to distance itself from the specifics of the industry and instead think more generally about the relationship between sex, harm, morality and commerce. Why is "good" sex intimate, private, romantic, and "bad" sex commercial, promiscuous, transitory? This chapter has sought to unpack the specific issues of time and space as they relate to the inherent harm of the sex industry.

In doing so, this chapter has detailed the massive increase in the sex industry in terms of variety of services, increasing number of workers and clients, and exponential rise in income and expenditure. We have also touched on the shift that has occurred in sexual commerce from the public to the private arena, especially with the growth of information technology. In such an environment, the vast majority of the sex industry is now mostly invisible to law enforcement, policy makers and legislators.

However, the largest and most dramatic shift which we have sought to discuss involves changes in the notion of sexual intimacy more generally, and how this has impacted upon the acceptability of promiscuity in the public sphere and, with it, changed the sexual landscape of sexual relationships and the acceptability of the sex industry. With entertainment, advertising and tourism promoting sex as an unsentimental consumer choice, a different group of people have begun populating the sex industry as clients, consumers, producers and workers. Although the sex industry continues to draw those from the most disadvantaged groups in society – a theme we explore in more detail in chapter 10, where we engage with the harm of sex trafficking – it is also clear that the new "middle class" is also moving into the industry in greater numbers. Sexual commerce is becoming normalized, and this is set against what some are now considering a major modification to the social and sexual elements of society. In perhaps as significant a shift as that which occurred in the later nineteenth century, the spatial reorganization of intimate private life into a more public spectacle, whether on television, on holidays, over the internet or in advertising, signals a dissolving of the temporal construction of the private sphere as the only appropriate place for sex.

10

SEX TRAFFICKING

Introduction

In 2006, the Australian Broadcasting Commission (ABC) ran a documentary called Sex Slaves on its premier current affairs programme, *Four Corners*. Produced as The Real Sex Traffic by Channel 4 in the UK, this documentary followed the journey of Viorel to find his pregnant wife, Katia, who had been kidnapped and sold to a gang of international sex traffickers for US$1000. According to the summary of the documentary on the *Four Corners* website (www.abc.net.au/4corners):

> Viorel embarks on a mission to free Katia from the pimp who now owns her in Turkey. Hidden cameras accompany him, capturing some of the traffickers, pimps and middlemen who buy and sell hundreds of thousands of women each year. Lured by the predators who exploit their naivete and dreams of employment abroad, many of these women are kidnapped and forced into sex slavery. They are sold to pimps, locked in brothels, drugged, terrorised and raped.
>
> Viorel enlists help from Vlad, the man who first sold Katia, who gives him the pimp's phone number in Turkey. In an interview Vlad explains his actions and opens a window on the pitiless economy of the sex trafficker.
>
> "Debt bondage represents the money that a girl is told she has to work off. That amount is easily inflated if the pimp wants. That way, the debt never goes away and she continues to work … without ever receiving a penny", he says.
>
> Armed with the pimp's phone number as his only lead, Viorel poses as another sex trafficker to try to buy his wife back. As the phone negotiations build to a crucial meeting, which is secretly filmed, other trafficked women explain what Katia might be enduring. "We worked for as long as we had clients, 24 hours a day. If we refused to service a client, they beat us up", says Tania about her captivity in Turkey. As the story of Viorel and Katia reaches its

remarkable conclusion, "Sex Slaves" exposes the official neglect that allows this abominable trade to flourish.

This programme beats a familiar drum: there is the innocent, young victim, the evil (foreign) trafficker and pimp, and the loving family. In the public psyche, victims of trafficking are all such vulnerable women and children, forced from the safety of their homes into gross sexual exploitation, and subject to the whims of degenerate men. This understanding has a very similar ring to fears in the nineteenth century about the white slave trade, where young white girls were thought to be in constant danger from the animal lusts of non-European men. In the twenty-first century, the direction has shifted from white western women to women from the developing world, specifically Eastern Europe and Asia. It is these women who are the new sex slaves.

But how accurate is this picture of modern illegal migration in the sex industry, and what other explanations are available to explain both the incidence of sex trafficking and the concomitant "cultural paranoia"? While the number of women and children trafficked for commercial sex work is impossible to quantify, national and international sources seem to agree that the global sex trade has increased substantially over the past fifteen years.[1] Certainly, in any market there are demand and supply forces at work. As discussed in chapter 9, the increasing use of technology in the commercialization of sex, as well as the shift to a recreational sexual ethic, has increased demand in the new sexual entertainment industries, and some of this demand is being satisfied by women from developing nations – a proportion of whom are trafficked. Whether they are fully aware of the work that awaits them, whether they are already working as prostitutes, or whether they are deceived, coerced or forced to illegally migrate for sex work, the UN estimates that this portion of the global sex industry generates US$7 billion profit annually.[2] Ironically, it is the large amounts of money involved in the global sex industry that generate the supply of women in the first place, accompanied by the feminization of poverty, the lack of employment opportunities for women in many countries, the rise of displaced persons during the 1990s, and the sale of western glamour via a global media. By unpacking the layers of harm within the global phenomenon of illegal migration, this chapter examines in detail the range of ways in which women come to work in the sex industry away from home, and analyses the western response. We question implicit and explicit attributions of harm to such work, the relationship of harm to women in particular, and the ways that western governments use these attributions to police borders.

Sex trafficking as a global phenomenon

Concern over the phenomenon of sex trafficking has been growing steadily over the past thirty years, but the twenty-first century has seen sex trafficking reach new heights of national and international attention. The clandestine gains made from trafficking in women and girls are estimated by some to exceed those made from the underground trade of arms and narcotics.[3] In the media, sex trafficking is now proclaimed as a multi-million-dollar underground industry and, along with terrorism and drug trafficking, one of three major concerns for governments internationally.[4]

This was borne out between 2000 and 2003, when the United Nations *Convention against Transnational Organized Crime* was accompanied by the *Protocol to Prevent, Suppress and Punish Trafficking in Persons Especially Women and Children*. Here trafficking was defined as:

> The recruitment, transportation, transfer, harbouring or receipt of persons, by means of the threat or use of force or other forms of coercion, of abduction, of fraud, of deception, of the abuse of power or of a position of vulnerability or of the giving or receiving of payments or benefits to achieve the consent of a person having control over another person, for the purpose of exploitation.[5]

For sex trafficking in particular, exploitation includes, at a minimum, the exploitation of the prostitution of others, and herein lies the problem: when is prostitution exploitation, and when is it emancipation or at least independence? When is prostitution forced, and when is it voluntary? When is one person's "rescue from exploitation" another person's "interrupted employment contract"?[6] If you are of the opinion that all prostitution is violence against women, there can be no voluntary prostitution because consent is meaningless. In this view, all prostitution is exploitation. Since all prostitution is coerced, all migration, both within and between borders for the purposes of prostitution, comes under the definition of trafficking. Internationally, this position is supported by the *Coalition Against Trafficking in Women*.[7]

If, on the other hand, you believe that prostitution can be a valid and rational occupational choice for women, then there is a clear difference between adult women who illegally migrate or are smuggled into a country for the purposes of prostitution, and those who are forced, coerced or deceived into migrating for the same purpose. In such cases, the distinction between forced and voluntary prostitution is a valid one, and only the former includes trafficking. This position is supported at international level by the *Global Alliance Against Traffic in Women*.[8] This is also the current position of the United Nations.

Obviously, such definitional differences have a major impact on how trafficking is identified, especially as the data on sex trafficking vary widely. For example, in the same year that the FBI estimated 700,000 women and children were trafficked worldwide – 2001 – UNICEF estimated 1.75 million, and the International Organization for Migration 500,000. Also in 2001, the UN drastically changed its own estimate of trafficked people – from 4,000,000 to 1,000,000, and again in 2010, to between 600,000 and 800,000.[9] Victims of sexual exploitation in Germany range from 2000 to 20,000, while in Russia estimates are from 10,000 to 100,000.[10] In Australia, numbers of sexually trafficked persons range from ten to 1000,[11] and in the USA they are estimated at from 14,500 to 50,000.[12] The most cited statistics on sex trafficking come from the US Department of State's *Annual Trafficking in Persons Report*.[13] According to the 2006 report, 600,000 to 800,000 people are trafficked across international borders each year, 80 per cent of whom are believed to be women and up to 50 per cent children. It is argued that the majority of these trafficked persons are for the purposes of sexual exploitation.[14]

The variation in these figures is partly to do with the definition of trafficking, especially the conflation of figures for sex trafficking with those for human smuggling and illegally migrating for the purposes of prostitution. Thus "in some accounts, all undocumented migrants assisted in their transit across national borders are counted as having been trafficked. In others, all migrant sex workers are defined as trafficking victims regardless of consent and conditions of labour."[15] These variable statistics are also related to the population under scrutiny: illegal, transient people. Victims may be hesitant to provide information or cooperate with authorities out of fear of reprisals for themselves or their families. There is also a blurring between smuggling and trafficking for many people, especially where large, undocumented, irregular labour migration is a common occurrence, as for example in South East Asia.[16] In such cases, "victims" may not perceive themselves as part of a trafficking problem.

Even the methodology used by the US State Department to access its annual figures remains unclear, according to the Australian Government Accountability Office.[17] "Rough estimates" of people trafficked into the sex industry thus tend to rely on extrapolations from secondary sources, "including non-government organisation surveys, estimates by police, sex workers and journalists as well as information from diplomatic agencies and key informants".[18] As such, all statistics on sex trafficking should be treated with caution.

When official statistics are available, they identify very small numbers: sixty-six sex trafficking victims were officially recognized by the Australian Government between 2004 and 2006.[19] In the USA between 1999 and 2000, there were thirty-eight documented cases of sex trafficking involving 5500 women.[20] These low official numbers have not deterred governments from legislating against trafficking and/or resourcing the fight. Since 2003, Australia has enacted new Federal offences to criminalize trafficking, and committed AUS$46.3 million to support initiatives to combat trafficking in persons.[21] The USA passed the *Victims of Trafficking and Violence Protection Act* in 2000; in 2001 the Economic Community of West African States (ECOWAS) passed its *Declaration and Action Plan on Human Trafficking;* in 2002 the South Asian Association for Regional Cooperation (SAARC) enacted the *Convention on Preventing and Combating Trafficking in Women and Children for Prostitution;* in 2002 the Council of the European Union proclaimed the *Directive on Short Term Residence Permits for Victims of Trafficking;* and the Philippines *Anti-Trafficking in Persons Act* was passed in 2003.[22] All support the UN Protocol on Trafficking and thus emphasize a growing concern about trafficking in general, and sex trafficking in particular.

The harm of sex trafficking

When governments legislate to fight trafficking across their borders, they are partly motivated to protect the human rights of the victims. This harm discourse is very important in the increasingly punitive discussion about trafficking, especially the identification and rescue of its victims. The similarity between twenty-first-century concerns over sex trafficking and nineteenth-century concerns about the white slave trade has not gone unnoticed in the literature: the focus on the innocence of the women and children involved; the vilification of the traffickers; the unsubstantiated claims; and the conflation of illegal migration, smuggling and trafficking. By discussing the harm of sex trafficking in the context of debates in the nineteenth century, we will confront what appears to be an ongoing cultural paranoia over the movement of women across borders.

The nineteenth century: white slave trade

According to Doezema,[23] the typical story of white slavery "involved white adolescent girls who were drugged and abducted by sinister immigrant procurers waking up to find themselves captive in some infernal foreign brothel where they were subject to the pornographic whims of sadistic non-white pimps and brothel masters". In *Pitfalls for Women*, published in the late nineteenth century, a few individual case histories described the ways in which "English girls are victimised – girls who are as pure as the dew, that sparkles on the grass at the first blush of dawn in the spring".[24] The cover of another contemporary publication, *In the Grip of the White Slave Trader*, has "an innocent girl in a white dress who, looking distressed and big eyed, is held fiercely by a massive hand around her torso".[25] A number of highly publicized exposés, including "The maiden tribute of modern Babylon" by W.T. Stead, published in the *Pall Mall Gazette* in 1885, served to heighten paranoia about the slave trade and focus public attention on the issue by documenting the sale of hundreds of young English girls to "aristocratic old rakes" both at home and abroad. The involvement of deceit, coercion and drugs, and the accusation that poor parents were selling their daughters to white slave traders, served only to heighten anxiety and attracted more than 250,000 people to Hyde Park in protests aimed at raising the age of consent from thirteen to sixteen. They succeeded.[26]

An important part of the campaign against the white slave trade was thus to create public sympathy for the victims. This could only be done if all responsibility for their predicament was removed. It was crucial to stress the level of deceit involved as well as the drugging, kidnapping and abduction. The various measures employed to achieve their innocence in the situation included emphasizing "her youth and/or her virginity, her whiteness and her unwillingness to be a prostitute".[27] In fact, it was this related image of child prostitution, exploited by Stead in "The maiden tribute", that gave impetus to the campaign against the white slave trade as the two issues became inextricably linked in the popular imagination in the UK, Europe and the USA, where "innocent country girls were lured to the dangerous and corrupt city".[28]

The linking of white slavery and child prostitution had all the symptoms of "cultural paranoia", despite the fact that evidence for widespread involuntary prostitution of British girls at home or abroad was slim.[29] During the 1870s and 1880s, officials were able to uncover a small traffic in women between Britain and Europe, although the women "lured" into licensed brothels in Antwerp and Brussels, for example, were by no means the young innocents depicted in the sensational stories. Similarly, there undoubtedly were some child prostitutes on the streets of London and elsewhere, but here too their numbers were grossly exaggerated. Nor were most of these children the victims of false entrapment, as "The maiden tribute" and other media stories of the time would suggest. Rather, what was discovered at the time was that missing girls rarely outnumbered missing boys, the numbers were small, and most were found and returned to their homes or to institutions.[30]

Another element in the paranoia over white slavery was the large numbers of people who were on the move in the later nineteenth century. Due in part to "large scale international relocations, and massive displacements of people that followed the abolition of slavery in the nineteenth century and which accompanied the internationalisation of waged labour embedded in the period between 1850 and 1914",[31] it exacerbated racist concerns over foreign men and white women travelling alone. Certainly, anti-slavery campaigners were keen to rescue single young women, and leaflets and posters were produced at ports and stations to warn girls off venturing abroad or to the city. If the numbers provided by the Federation of National Unions for the Protection of Girls can be believed, 27,000 travelling girls annually were accommodated in 518 homes at the end of the nineteenth century in England alone, thus suggesting support for a population on the move.[32]

What is certainly clear is that this fear and concern over the harm of white slavery influenced high-level international interest in the issue. In the five years before the end of the nineteenth century, three international conferences were held on the prevention of trafficking in women, as well as the first congress on the white slave trade. The shocking revelations that "women, for the most part under age, were engaged for lucrative posts, and then, always in complete ignorance of the abominable lot which awaited them, transported to foreign countries and finally flung penniless into houses of debauchery" fitted with these earlier understandings, and by the early years of the twentieth century, two international instruments concerning the trade had been created.[33]

When the League of Nations was created after the First World War, it adopted these two earlier conventions, but shifted discussion from the "white slave trade" to "traffic in women and children" and offered a third and fourth convention of its own in 1921 and 1933. These later conventions included attempted as well as actual procurement, and broadened the offence of procurement to women who had consented *without force or deceit*.[34] This crucial shift in the understanding of trafficking meant that many more women could be identified as trafficked, since it was now defined as "direct or indirect procuration and transportation for gain to a foreign country of women and girls for the sexual gratification of one or more other persons".[35] For example, in 1927 in Buenos Aires, it was reported that 4500 foreign prostitutes worked in the city, and that 75 per cent of them were trafficked because "they did not travel on their own initiative but rather went at the behest of their pimp".[36]

> Once a foreign girl is taken to a distant country where she does not understand the language and customs, and is far from her home and friends, the power of the trafficker is proportionately increased and she is accordingly a better subject

for intimidation than local girls. Herein lies the studied cruelty and slavery which inevitably follows the international traffic.[37]

Such an understanding served to destabilize the independent decision-making of the women involved, as well as to offer a relationship between domestic and international prostitution. Certainly, many feminists opposed the regulation of prostitution in their home country, believing it to be the institutionalization of male vice and the legalization of a class of women to service the uncontrolled lust of men. However, in the campaign against white slavery, the regulation of domestic prostitution was also seen as the basis for pimps and traffickers to gain access to white women.

In 1949, the UN adopted the *Convention for the Suppression of the Traffic in Persons and of the Exploitation of the Prostitution of Others*, which combined and superseded the earlier conventions. "It declared that prostitution and trafficking was incompatible with the dignity and worth of the human person and endangered the welfare of the individual, the family and the community."[38] It is notable in that it did not differentiate between forced and voluntary prostitution, or between children and adults, or between domestic and international procurement. In fact, it did not even specifically define trafficking, but it did require signatory countries to "work to prevent prostitution, to dismantle legal brothels, and to rehabilitate the victims of prostitution".[39] By dissolving the distinctions between child and adult prostitution and forced and voluntary prostitution, the distinction between prostitution and sex trafficking was also removed.

Twentieth/twenty-first century: trafficking of innocents

The 2003 media stories of Puangthong Simaplee, a twenty-seven-year-old Thai woman who died while confined at the Villawood Detention Centre outside Sydney, Australia while awaiting deportation, demonstrate the continuity between nineteenth- and twenty-first-century understandings of sex trafficking in the popular imagination. According to media stories at the time, Simaplee was detained after immigration officers discovered her during a raid on a Sydney brothel. Her media portrayal as a woman who had been enslaved as a prostitute from the age of twelve not only gained the journalists who detailed her plight a 2003 Human Rights Award (print media category), but is credited with motivating the Australian Federal Government to bring legislation and anti-trafficking policy in line with the newly created international standards, particularly the 2003 *UN Protocol to Prevent, Suppress and Punish Trafficking in Persons Especially Women and Children*.[40]

Such images of trafficked women dominate in the media, political debates and the academic literature. The stories involve young women, tricked into moving away from home and family, lured by false promises of earning substantial amounts of money in exotic locations. Once they arrive to work in the promised bar, restaurant or as a house maid or nanny for a wealthy family, they instead have their passport taken and are forced into prostitution to repay the costs of the illegal travel.

> Lena, aged 21, was recruited by a woman who said her daughter was working in Greece and making a lot of money. When Lena arrived in Greece, her passport was taken away and she was put into a small room in a brothel, guarded by two dogs. She was sold in prostitution each night from 9 in the evening until 6 in the morning. When she escaped and returned to Mykolayiv, she had US $55.00.[41]

Trafficking is consistently linked with slavery, but is argued to be a far more serious problem than in the past. "Four centuries of slavery moved about 11.5 million people out of Africa. While in the last decade more than 30 million women and children may have been trafficked."[42] Not only is it argued that huge numbers of women and children are involved in this modern slave trade, but that the traffickers treat their victims similarly to the slave traders. Women are stripped, displayed and auctioned, and extreme violence is used to control them. In Istanbul it was reported that "two women were thrown off a balcony and killed while six of their Russian friends watched", while in Serbia "a woman was beheaded in public". It is maintained that such punishments are regularly meted out to trafficked women who refuse to engage in prostitution, and serve as a warning to others.[43]

An important part of this image of victimization is not only the victims' innocence, and the deceit, but their unwillingness to work as prostitutes and/or their lack of experience in prostitution. Much is made in exposés of trafficking on the process of "breaking in" these women, a process where women are raped and beaten upon their arrival in the destination country "in order to break the woman's will and to impress upon them their powerlessness … the rape also teaches women how to do prostitution sex".[44] The importance of innocence in this picture is crucial to their victimization, but there is much sleight of hand in presenting the trafficked victim as childlike. In a 1995 UNICEF report, it was noted that "the number of Myanmar girls working in Thai brothels has been conservatively estimated at between 20,000 and 30,000 with approximately 10,000 new recruits brought in yearly. The majority are between 12 and 25 years old." There was no indication of what proportion were under eighteen and thus actually girls as opposed to women.[45]

While there is some recognition that the majority of women trafficked into prostitution are aware of the work they will be doing in their destination country, such women are "coated with a dusting of victimisation to make them more palatable".[46] In such cases, the "knowing trafficking victim" is rendered innocent by the invocation of her poverty and desperation.

> One of thousands of women from Thailand, the Philippines, Malaysia and China trafficked to Australia and other First World Countries by crime syndicates each year, Susie is the face of contemporary poverty. That her job as a debt bonded sex worker is the best economic option available to her is a metaphor for most of the world's women, whose grinding impoverishment in the Third World is accelerating.[47]

Victimization is also alluded to by focusing on refugee camps for displaced persons as "providing a ready pool of vulnerable women and children to be recruited into the global sex industry".[48]

Innocent, naive and desperate in these accounts are code for "non-prostitute". So what happens when the innocent victim, constructed to appeal to the public and policy makers as a sexually blameless young woman, is revealed to be outside the persona of the trafficked innocent? Interestingly, this exact scenario occurred in Australia, when a later media exposé revealed a different life journey for Simaplee, the trafficking victim noted earlier. In this alternative biography, Simaplee was portrayed as a young woman who travelled for work and adventure, entering Australia voluntarily at the age of twenty-one "to see the happy life".[49] Photos produced by her parents, which show her in the Snowy Mountains, on Bondi Beach, in Melbourne and on Sydney Harbour, certainly put paid to the myth of her imprisonment, which was much touted in the earlier stories. However, while the truth of Simaplee's plight is unclear, what is clear is that this second story would not have motivated a government to change its policy and legislation to protect victims of trafficking. As Saunders[50] correctly identifies:

> The story of a helpless migrant woman sold as a child into prostitution can become part of a successful campaign to change a nation's laws while the story of a young woman who travelled for adventure and a better life cannot.

This "tale of two Simaplees" highlights the problems of using myth and cultural paranoia to understand a very real and complex problem. The distinctions between trafficking and smuggling, between coercion and consent, are muddied when we discuss the harm of illegal migration into the sex industry. However, these distinctions do have real consequences for the women and children involved. In Germany, for example, the penalty for trafficking is reduced when a woman knows she is going to be a prostitute or is deemed "not far from being a prostitute". Other countries, including Columbia, Uganda, Canada, Japan and Brazil, have similar provisions.[51] In the Netherlands, police will refuse to investigate complaints of trafficking by women who continue working as prostitutes.[52] In the USA, legislation to protect victims of trafficking relies heavily on the distinction between innocent victims of forced prostitution and guilty sex workers who had foreknowledge of the fact that they would be performing sexual labour. Victims of sex trafficking are not "ordinary abused migrants", but rather those who "are found behind dark, padlocked doors and hidden corridors. The deprivations of food, the beating with electrical wires, metal rods, and leather straps, the cigarette burns and the brutal rapes are conducted in the hidden rooms."[53] Such extreme portrayals have allowed action to be taken against sexual slavery while leaving in place policies that continue to punish the majority of ordinary prostitutes and abused and exploited illegal migrants.

Such portrayals also serve to hide the exploitation, deceit and coercion that can occur when women knowingly and willingly travel illegally into a country to work as prostitutes. These women are not the forced, innocent and naive victims of the trafficking myth. They may have willingly paid their "trafficker", they may already work as a prostitute in their country of origin, and they may understand they will have to work for a time in the debt bondage of a brothel. When they arrive, they may not have their passport confiscated, but they may find that their debt is far greater than they agreed, that they will have no choice in their clients, and that the hours they must work are excessive. "It is one thing to save innocent victims of trafficking, quite another to recognise that guilty sex workers deserve respect for their rights as workers, as women and as migrants."[54]

Migrating for work

Trafficking can be examined outside the cultural paranoia and myth as part of a bigger story of travelling for work. In 2005, the UN estimated that 3 per cent of the world's population were migrants (191 million) and that 30–40 million might be unauthorized.[55] The same report also estimated that women currently constitute more than half of all migrants, both legal and illegal, and that "women who accept the challenge of migration worldwide are increasingly motivated by the desire for personal betterment as well as, or even rather than, by family responsibilities".[56] Such statistics are to be placed in the context of a recent report by the International Labour Organization, which estimated that around 30 per cent of the world's labour force is unemployed and unable to sustain a minimum standard of living.

Travelling for employment has a long history. "In the nineteenth century, large numbers of women migrated from Europe and Russia to the Americas, South Africa, other parts of Europe and Asia, in part supported by British colonialism and facilitated by new technology, especially the steamship and telegraph".[57] From the late twentieth century, we have been witness to the "largest mass migration in human history" due to the reconfiguration of the global economy, an increased ability to travel, the displacement and dispossession of marginalized people, an awareness of better options, armed conflict, and an aspiration to explore the world.[58] "Women have figured largely in this recent mass migration and are mostly employed on a contractual basis as foreign domestic workers in the maid trade".[59]

Travelling to sell sex has always been associated with itinerancy. Throughout history, women accompanied campaigning soldiers and pilgrims, and by the nineteenth century, women from Europe and Russia dominated the prostitute population in Buenos Aires. At the same time, 25 per cent of the registered prostitutes in Italy were migrants, 15 per cent of prostitutes in Russia were migrants, and British women were found working across Europe.[60] In the late twentieth/early twenty-first centuries, migrants selling sex are found travelling in every possible direction. By the 1980s, up to 60 per cent of the women working as prostitutes in the Netherlands were from Latin America and Asia; by the 1990s, 70 per cent of the prostitutes in Japan were reported to be from the Philippines. Afghan and Bangladeshi women can be found working as prostitutes in Pakistan; in India, the prostitute workforce currently includes women from Nepal; women from Eastern Europe, Russia and Vietnam can be found working in China; Thai prostitutes work in Australia; Russian women in Egypt; Ghanaians in Austria; Nigerians in Senegal; Italian and Polish women in Germany.[61]

It is also clear that the vast majority of migrants who travel to work in the sex industry know early on that their work will have a sexual component. This has been documented in Australia,[62] northern and southern Europe,[63] the USA[64] and Japan.[65] While knowing beforehand does not mean that exploitation and unhappiness will not occur, migrants also widely understand that migration carries with it risks and dangers. "Women in Nairobi who were asked if they realised that sex jobs could be dangerous, answered that they were not selling sex in order to live safely but to earn money and be independent."[66]

However, it would be incorrect to infer that economics is the only reason why people migrate. Desire, pleasure, romance, risk, adventure and the opportunity for a new life all feature in stories of migration:

> I worked in a company, but they were letting people go. I had problems with my children's father, he mistreated me, he threatened me, they were going to fire me. I have a sister who's a resident here … I came with the money they gave me when they threw me out of work (Ecuadorian woman in Spain).[67]

> Sometimes I enjoy working, I can travel and see beautiful places. I can go to nice restaurants. I enjoy that the Turkish men view us as desirable (Ukrainian woman in Turkey).[68]

To be able to migrate, two options are available: to arrive with legal documentation, or to arrive illegally. Given that most people migrate to create a better life for themselves and their families, they need to earn money. However, many migrants cannot gain access to the formal economy in the destination country. This may be because they do not have the appropriate or required skills or qualifications; because their qualifications aren't recognized in the destination country; or because the destination country limits the number of foreign workers in their particular trade or job. Since work permits are generally difficult to obtain, and for citizens of many countries accessing even a tourist visa can be difficult, or may require years of waiting, illegal migration to work in the informal sector of a country may be the only option.[69]

The informal economy comprises that work which is not recognized by government accounting – it is tax-free – and includes do-it-yourself work; guarding parking spaces; bet-running; providing bed and breakfast; begging; selling food, sunglasses, produce, leather goods; carpentry and construction services; nannying and domestic labour. It is a vast, unregulated, unprotected economic sector of society, and includes both legal and illegal workers in its midst.[70] Perhaps not surprisingly, women are disproportionally represented in informal economies worldwide, based as they are on flexible employment conditions. Moreover, an increasingly globalized economy has seen many women migrate to seize economic opportunities overseas, where, for example, the Philippines has put more women into the global workforce than any other country.[71] In the case of migration, informal work may be the only available way of making a living. Certainly, jobs selling sex are a part of the informal sector in all countries worldwide, but laws prohibiting or regulating prostitution and migration combine to create highly complex and often oppressive situations for women if they become involved in prostitution once abroad. For example, in countries where prostitution is legal, such employment opportunities are not extended to foreign workers or illegal immigrants.[72]

There are therefore few legal and independent ways to migrate in the informal sector, and as a consequence migrants are forced to make use of intermediaries or middlemen who sell information, services and documents. When migrants cannot afford to buy these outright, they go into debt. Those who sell these services are often family members, old friends, tourist acquaintances or independent entrepreneurs, and the services they offer include passports, visas, work permits, advice, money, transportation, lodgings and contact with potential employers. What is clear is that the decision to take such a journey requires these networks, and this in turn relies on social as well as economic capital. Such networks are also not difficult to find in countries where "out travel" is normal, and they may even be part of the formal sector, for example, in travel agencies.[73]

> Hari-Prar arranged my illegal documents. It took him months, many trips to Chandigarh and Delhi and cost me everything Prakash had saved. My passport name, officially, was Jyoti Vijh. My date of birth made me safely nineteen years old. "Otherwise problems" said the travel advisors. All over Punjab, travel agents are willing to advise (Indian nanny in New York).[74]

These networks are not new, but they have been criticized *en masse* since the cultural paranoia over sex trafficking. The irony is that immigration into wealthy countries is very restricted while, paradoxically, a demand exists for these workers – especially for women in domestic labour, as marriage partners and in the sex and entertainment industry. There is also a differentiation of treatment based on country of origin, where, in Australia for example, young women from the UK and Canada have no problem getting working visas while young women from South East Asia are denied such access.[75] While this differential treatment is partly informed by bilateral agreements between governments, it is also the case that Australian immigration officials deported eighty young Thai women in two years under *Operation Paper Tiger*.[76]

Such differential immigration policies can also be situated within the more general discussion of forced versus voluntary prostitution. In this case, the victim of trafficking is part of a much bigger set of concerns that differentiate along racial lines.

> The voluntary prostitute is a Western sex worker, seen as capable of making independent decisions about whether or not to sell sexual services, while the sex worker from a developing country is deemed unable to make the same choice: she is passive, naive and ready prey for traffickers.[77]

The non-western woman is positioned as "ignorant, poor, uneducated, tradition bound, domestic, family orientated, victimised". She is not yet a "whole or developed person", but instead resembles "a minor needing guidance, assistance and help". This construct then stands in opposition to a western woman who is believed to have

(or have the potential for) "control over her income, body and sexuality: the eman-
cipated, independent post-modern woman".[78]

This image of the victim of trafficking rests on the role of the west as "rescuer".
However, once rescued, the majority of trafficked women and girls are not allowed
to stay in the destination country. Rather, they are returned home as undocumented
migrants, left to face the shame and humiliation that accompanies such categorization
and status. In addition, there is the fear of reprisals from traffickers, or the concern
that the woman's family or home community will be made aware of her involvement
in criminalized, stigmatized activities. These women also return to the same situation
that prompted their migration, smuggling or trafficking in the first place, and as a
consequence newly returned or deported migrants may simply make new attempts to
leave. They become once again vulnerable to smuggling, deception or coercion in
the migration process.[79]

The trafficking discourse tends to rely on the notion that poor women are better
off staying at home than leaving and possibly getting into trouble. Efforts to prevent
trafficking thus focus on preventing migration, but the money that migrants send
home not only contributes to individual families, but now represents a large proportion of many countries' gross domestic product. For example, the World Bank estimated that migrant remittances to developing countries reached almost $80 billion in
2002, and these exceeded the net foreign direct investment for the first time. Poorer
countries thus have little interest in controlling outward movement, either legal or
illegal, and embassies and consulates will often grant spurious visas.[80]

Perhaps unfortunately, in a climate of cultural paranoia over transnational crime,
people-smuggling and terrorism, the courage and initiative required to change one's
life circumstances through migration is ignored in the desire to see all illegal migration
as the result of deceit, coercion and exploitation. What is needed is safe migration. In
this way, the violation and injustices in the current process could be eliminated and
the right to freedom of movement guaranteed for all. "People don't want to be rescued, they want to be safe. They don't want to go back, they want to go on".[81]
While migration for prostitution brings with it its own specific issues and problems
for the women concerned, its central elements are still about independence and
economic opportunity.

Conclusion

A friend proposed that I come, she knew a girl who could bring me ... You
sign a note for 7 million pesos (4207 Euros) and they tell you that you can pay
it back working for a month. You know what you're going to be doing.
Anyone who said she didn't know, it's a lie – a married lady with children,
how can she not know what she is going to be doing here? When you arrive
you crash, because the work is bad and it's a lie that the debt can be paid in a
month. You talk with the other girls and see that the debt is more than it cost
the girl to bring you. But you want to pay her because she takes a risk too, to
bring you over (Columbian woman in Spain).[82]

I was deceived. On arriving I began to rebel and the problems began. The first few days they made me come down and I sat in a chair and wanted to throw stones at the drunks that came near me. Then the guy told me: look, things can't go on like this, you owe me 33 000 pesetas (1800 Euros) that you have to pay me with your work here. Everyone owes me that money and all work to pay me. When you pay me, you can leave (Columbian woman in Spain).[83]

To return to the provinces and to live as poorly as your parents would be like dying. So there is no choice! You have to pay for your right to live in the capital, to have a good job and a flat with what you have got. With your body ... today thousands of girls are calmly and calculatedly selling themselves. The stupider ones do it just for the money, those with more brains and bigger plans do it for a prestigious job and a place to live (Russian woman in Moscow).[84]

I left my job in the Ukraine because it was boring there. I wanted to go abroad and experience the world. After my experience in Italy I came to Turkey two years ago because I was looking for a chance ... When I came to Turkey I didn't know about the opportunity to work as a sex worker. I first worked as a translator in Karakoy (Ukrainian woman in Turkey).[85]

Each of these women has travelled to work in prostitution, either within their national borders or outside them. They represent a continuum of the various ways in which women move to work in the global sex industry. Their voices thus offer a challenge to the dominant representations of trafficked women from less developed countries who are naive and sexually innocent, and who move only through desperate poverty. These women have ambition and seek adventure, they show spirit and ingenuity. This is not to argue, of course, that a proportion of women who leave their homes and end up working as prostitutes are not desperately harmed, exploited and oppressed. Quite deliberately, this discussion has also avoided any discussion of the movement of children for sex work. Following the UN, we are of the opinion that children do not belong in the global sex industry and that their consent is irrelevant. However, this is not the case with women, whose consent is a crucial issue, and this can challenge the representation of them as victims, even when deceit or coercion is evident. Many women who are legitimately identified as "victims of trafficking" do not always want to embrace such a label, preferring instead to see themselves as "a migrant worker who has had some bad luck as the result of a bad decision".[86]

This rejection of the status of victim is a crucial challenge to the current anti-trafficking position, which tends to see many women who migrate to work, in the sex industry and elsewhere, as passive and often stupid, certainly naive actors in their own life-course. Returning them home, of course, places them back in the same situation as previously, and does not go any way towards identifying why they moved in the first place. It also does nothing to make their next migration any safer and redirects attention from the ways in which the governments of wealthy countries tighten their borders while demand for the services offered by legal and illegal migrants increases.

11

CONCLUSION

The process of writing this book has been both enlightening and sobering. Our goal was to explore the nexus between sex, crime and morality via the development of new theoretical frameworks, and in doing so we have touched on many issues, some of them in depth, but many of them only cursorily. It has been difficult to identify just which issues should be addressed in the context and limitations of this monograph, and which must be set aside for future attention, frustrating as that may be. Our use of historical, philosophical, social, legal and feminist discourses as tools for identifying the underlying assumptions we have about sex and crime has allowed us to analyse the associated values, beliefs and mores. However, each case study only touches on some of the possible points of discussion, and we acknowledge that much more could have been said on each topic. Nevertheless, our theoretical explorations have led us to some remarkable conclusions, and we hope that the foregoing has presented some challenges to existing thinking about sex and crime, and provided a way forward for new understandings in the field.

For example, in May 2010 *The Weekend Australian*, Australia's only national newspaper, ran a pithy sexuality report in its magazine entitled "Who needs a man?" arguing that an increasing number of young women are describing themselves as bisexual or lesbian. The report cites a Cornell study of 20,000 young people from 2007, which found that 14.4 per cent of young American women claimed to be lesbian or bisexual; a New Zealand study, which put the figure at 16.4 per cent; and another study in Norway, which estimated that nearly 20 per cent of young women and girls identified as lesbian or bisexual. How do we explain such a shift in the sexual ethic of young women, especially since, as this report maintains, male homosexuality has been stable at 4–5 per cent since the 1950s?

One explanation is a shift in the sexual ethics of Generation Y, with the public performance of sexuality and the rise of a recreational sexual ethic both gaining ground in the twenty-first century for this new generation of sexually active young people. Ironically, it is also this group of young people who appear to practise a sexual ethic that we of Generation X and the Baby Boomers cannot really comprehend, and who have been the object of the most prurient social policing of childhood sexuality. Thus the first and most provocative finding of our research has been the existence of numerous unrecognized contradictions in and between current discourses surrounding sex in general, and sex crimes in particular. On one hand, for example, there appear to be greater discursive explorations of sex and a general reinterpretation of the boundaries of acceptability in terms of sexual practices and beliefs about sex, especially in the public sphere. Chapter 9, for example, notes the rise of compensated dating, which articulates an up-front understanding of the benefits to be gained by attractive young women in a society that both desires youth and beauty and offers women a status through it, not to mention the surprising announcement that "oral sex is the new kiss" – thus once again shifting the boundaries of normal sexual practice among the young. Similarly, chapter 7 found, in its explorations of public perceptions of sexuality, a decided shift in the acceptability of both non-heterosexual and non-normative sexual practices such as bondage and domination. Clearly, society is becoming more open to sexuality and sexual possibilities that once were silenced, or at least kept behind closed doors. There seems to be almost a celebration of alternative or deviant sexualities – a finding that is both heartening and hopeful – as well as a definitive recognition that society ought to find a place for the different and othered. That young women can make out with each other in bars without fear of censure – indeed, to the delight of their boyfriends and girlfriends alike – and that parliaments are debating gay rights, suggests an opening up of attitudes in ways that have not occurred for several centuries, at least in the west.

All this new public sex talk and behaviour, however, is counterbalanced by a corresponding closing of minds towards, and narrowing of definitions of, what is considered to be bad sex. Never in history has there been a greater fear of what the wrong kind of sex can do to people, especially children. Never before have children and young people been regarded as so vulnerable to bad sex and sexuality in general. Never before has sex marked out so clearly the boundaries between childhood and adulthood. Thus we have seen media reports of campaigns aimed at regulating certain categories of sex offenders to the point of vigilantism, and a massive exaggeration of the danger children and young people face from such offenders. In spite of the fact that very few children are abducted by strangers,[1] those who are become the focus of media and criminal justice discourses to the point of causing ongoing cultural paranoia about child sexual abuse. This has not been helped by recent revelations of paedophilia within religious organizations. The sexual predator is everywhere, and we must school our children in "stranger danger" and other forms of personal safety. Children must be kept asexual and innocent, and whether or not this is a worthy goal, the corollary is that our children are being brought up to fear sex, sexuality and adults. On the other hand, the normal development of children toward adult sexuality is one of the crucial goals of parenting, and the failure of children to make the transition to successful sexual relationships as an adult not only fills an entire section in most bookshops in the western world, but is also one of the crucial markers of child sexual abuse.

The second contradiction lies in the way we think about disadvantage in our society. We note that more sustained attention is being paid towards marginalized groups such as sexual minorities, migrant women and women from low socio-economic backgrounds. Government policies concerning the trafficking of women from less developed countries aim to police the exploitation of young migrant women, and legislation is already in place in many western countries to ensure that the rights of non-heterosexuals, transgendered individuals and other sexual minorities are achieved. For example, the plight of young female migrants who have been trafficked for sexual commerce has achieved enormous media and political attention in recent times after many years of silent political and social toleration. And when the United Kingdom passed a law in 2005 to allow same-sex civil partnerships, it was a momentous occasion, the likes of which we never would have thought we'd see in our lifetimes. One only need look in the local newspaper to understand just how much we, as a society, are concerned with righting the wrongs arising out of class, gender and ethnic differences. As chapter 8 notes, in February 2010 there were over 100 stories in *The Guardian* about sex trafficking alone. Surely we have never been so caring, so keen to close the gaps between class, race and gender.

At the same time, however, these new discourses on equality and rights belie the fact of increasing homophobic violence that is still occurring in the west. While academics are championing queer issues, and parliaments are debating how best to address the exploitation of women from less developed countries, gay, lesbian and transgendered individuals are still being subjected to physical and emotional abuse, and ethnically diverse migrant women are being stopped and refused entry into western nations on the tenuous assumption that they may be objects of sexual exploitation. Chapters 7 and 10 point out that such contradictions suggest that equality discourses are merely deflecting attention from what is still a very real problem – the fact that our society continues to be divided by class, race, gender, ethnicity and sexuality. While the new discourses do go some way towards alleviating differences, much of the effect is lost because those discourses also serve to mask and even exacerbate ongoing disadvantage and marginalization. This is articulated most clearly in chapter 10, where we identify the difficulty in distinguishing between the trafficking, smuggling and illegal migration of sex workers. What we are able to identify, however, is the differing ways in which such people are discussed. In the twenty-first century, it is non-western women from the less developed and former communist countries who are most likely to be perceived as victims of trafficking. Western women are the voluntary prostitutes who are seen as making independent decisions about whether or not to sell sexual services, while sex workers from developing countries are viewed as unable to act as agents in their own lives or to make an uncoerced decision to work in the sex industry. It is only the latter who are victims of sex trafficking.

The continued over-legislating of sex and sex crimes in western societies gives the impression that bad sex, and the people who perpetrate it, are being policed and/or regulated in a way that will bring benefits to society as a whole. However, our current fear of sex offenders is a recent phenomenon, linked to shifts in the public culture of sex and changes in our perception of the body functionality of men and women. It is only since the nineteenth century that many of the crimes associated with sex have come into being, and certainly during the eighteenth century sex crimes did not have the same sense of violation of the self as they do now. This has had major impacts on the ways in which we police sex crimes, especially against those perceived as the most vulnerable in society – women and children. Moreover, the truth of the matter, as we have seen, is that the policing of sex offenders over and beyond their periods of incarceration has not led to a reduction in the incidence of sex offences. In addition, all this criminal justice and media attention to paedophilia and child sexual abuse – a crime that, we have noted, is relatively rare in our society – masks the kinds of concern to which we should really be paying attention. Kincaid remarks, for example, that while there are only around 100 child abductions every year in the United States, it has been estimated that almost 15 million children – that is, one in four – in that country live in poverty.[2] Moreover, there are many, many ways in which a child can be abused other than sexually. The child protection authorities in each of the western nations have access to reams of files on poor young children who have been neglected, physically injured or exploited by carers and their associates, and yet it is the abducted white child from the middle-class family who obtains the most attention. It is not until a child dies, it seems, that we consider the issue of non-sexual child abuse to be worthy of debate. Again, the current discourses on child safety and the danger of sexual predators give the impression of social empowerment while masking other, more pressing social issues. Sex sells, both politically and commercially, it seems.

Similarly, sex trafficking gets attention only at the extreme ends of the industry, when child abduction and bondage are at play. This masks the varying ways in which women come to migrate to western developed nations, and hides the deceit, abuse and exploitation of willing participants in the global sex trade. It also ignores the reasons why 40 million people are currently listed as illegal migrants by the UN, and the sexual exploitation in other areas of employment for illegal migrants, like the clothes industry and private domestic labour. There are also no opportunities for women to *legally* migrate from developing to developed economies when they work in the sex industry, despite the fact that such an industry may be legal in the country to which they wish to migrate. Finally, there is an increased amount of work being done by wealthy nations to tighten border controls and to keep out illegal migrants, and this makes smuggling and trafficking all the more desirable. So, where to go from here? How do we take this public openness towards sex talk and turn it into something positive, something that has an impact on disadvantage and marginalization, instead of merely leading us away from thinking constructively about such issues? We do not claim to have the answers to this question – much more research, especially empirical research, could be done on these issues, and we hope this book provides the impetus for others to step up to the plate in that regard. We do suggest, however, that to move forward we first need to acknowledge that our understandings about sex and sex crimes are much more complex and multilayered than we suspect, and that they contain contradictions that urgently need to be addressed. We also need to remove our collective heads from the sand to find ways of opening up public spaces that acknowledge and accept a variety of non-normative sexualities and sexual practices, rather than pretending either that they do not exist, or that we have already addressed them to our collective satisfaction. In doing so, we may go some small way to addressing the kinds of marginalization experienced by, for example, a majority of sex workers, non-heterosexuals and ethnically diverse migrant women, while at the same time opening up for honest debate the underlying assumptions we have about the dangers of sex, the predatory nature of non-normative sexualities, and the status of children's sexuality – all issues, as we have pointed out, that come with more baggage than we can comfortably live with.

NOTES

1 Introduction

1 Ms Stryker's blog can be accessed at http://purrversatility.blogspot.com (accessed 29 September 2011).
2 Jeffrey Weeks, 2007, *The World We Have Won: The Remaking of Erotic and Intimate Life*. London and New York, Routledge.
3 Andrea Dworkin, 1981, *Pornography: Men Possessing Women*. New York, Perigee Press.
4 Weeks, 2007, *op. cit.*, p. 10.
5 Laura Maria Agustin, 2007, *Sex at the Margins: Migration, Labour Markets and the Rescue Industry*. London and New York, Zed Books, p. 8.

2 Out of time: the moral temporality of sex and taboo

1 Clare Masters and Justin Vallejo, 2008, "Bill Hensen to be charged over child porn photographs," *The Courier Mail*, 24 May 2008.
2 Gallery of NSW: http://archive.artgallery.nsw.gov.au/sub/billhenson/exhibitions/press.html (accessed 29 September 2011).
3 *Pavement Magazine*, 2003, "Bill Henson", www.pavementmagazine.com/billhenson.html (accessed 29 September 2011).
4 www.billhenson.net.au (accessed 29 September 2011).
5 Judith Halberstam, 2005, *In a Queer Time and Place*. New York, New York University Press.
6 Halberstam, 2005, p. 1.
7 Phillipe Aries, 1973, *Centuries of Childhood*. Harmondsworth, Penguin.
8 David Newman and Rebecca Smith, 1999, *The Social Construction of Childhood*. Newbury Park, CA, Pine Forge Press.
9 Newman and Smith, 1999.
10 Newman and Smith, 1999.
11 Newman and Smith, 1999. See also Bruce Bellingham, 1988, "The history of childhood since the 'invention of childhood': some issues in the eighties", *Journal of Family History*, 13(1), 347–58.
12 Kerry Carrington with Margaret Periera, 2009, *Offending Youth: Sex, Crime and Justice*. Sydney, Federation Press.

13 EIU, 2008, *The Future of Higher Education: How Technology Will Shape Learning*. London, Economist Intelligence Unit.

14 EIU, 2008. See also AIHW, 2005, *Australia's Welfare 2005*, Cat. No. AUS65. Canberra, Australian Institute of Health and Welfare.

15 AVERT, 2009, "Worldwide ages of consent". www.avert.org/age-of-consent.htm (accessed 29 September 2011).

16 Matthew Waites, 2005, *The Age of Consent: Young People, Sexuality and Citizenship*. London, Palgrave Macmillan.

17 David Bennett, 2007, "Adolescent development and risk-taking", Youth Action and Policy Association, NSW. www.yapa.org.au/youthwork/young/devrisk.php (accessed 29 September 2011).

18 Karen L. Kinnear, 2007, *Child Sexual Abuse: A Reference Handbook*. Santa Barbara, CA, ABC-CLIO, Inc.

19 *The New York Times*, 1997, "Teacher guilty of rape for sex with student", Section A, p. 24, New York Edition. www.nytimes.com/1997/08/08/us/teacher-guilty-of-rape-for-sex-with-student.html (accessed 29 September 2011). For a detailed account of the case, see J. Robinson, 2001, *The Mary Kay Letourneau Affair*. Overland Park, KS, Leathers Publishing.

20 AVERT, 2009, "Worldwide ages of consent". www.avert.org/age-of-consent.htm (accessed 29 September 2011).

21 OHCHR, 1990, *Convention on the Rights of the Child*, Part 1, Article 19. Geneva, Office of the High Commissioner for Human Rights.

22 For a comprehensive overview of child abuse laws and policies in Australia, see Justin Healey (ed.), 2005, *Child Sexual Abuse*. Thirroul, NSW, Spinney Press. For a UK focus, see Julia Davidson, 2008, *Child Sexual Abuse: Media Representations and Government Reactions*. Hoboken, NJ, Taylor & Francis.

23 Elizabeth Grosz, 1994, *Volatile Bodies: Towards a Corporeal Feminism*. Indianapolis, IN, Indiana University Press, p. 35.

24 Grosz, 1994, p. 35.

25 Judith Butler, 1993, *Bodies That Matter: On the Discursive Limits of Sex*. New York, Routledge.

26 For an in-depth discussion of hegemonic femininity, see Judith Butler, 1990, *Gender Trouble*. New York, Routledge; and on masculinity, see R.W. Connell, 2005, *Masculinities*, 2nd edn. Crows Nest, NSW, Allen & Unwin.

27 Judith Halberstam, 1998, *Female Masculinity*. Durham, NC, Duke University Press.

28 Connell, 2005, *op. cit.*

3 Incest

1 Sybil Wolfram, 1987, *In-Laws and Out-Laws: Kinship and Marriage in England*. London, Croom Helm, p. 26.

2 Wolfram, 1987, p. 29.

3 Wolfram, 1987, p. 21.

4 Wolfram, 1987, p. 26.

5 Wolfram, 1987, p. 18.

6 Polly Morris, 1992, "Incest or survival strategy? Plebeian marriage within the prohibited degrees in Somerset, 1730–1835", in John Fout (ed.), *Forbidden History: The State, Society and the Regulation of Sexuality in Modern Europe*. Chicago, IL, University of Chicago Press, p. 140.

7 Morris, 1992, p. 144.

8 Morris, 1992, p. 140.

9 Morris, 1992, p. 156.

10 Morris, 1992, p. 142.

11 Morris, 1992, p. 142.

12 Wolfram, 1987, p. 40.

13 Wolfram, 1987, p. 42.

14 Morris, 1992, *op. cit.*, p. 157.

15 Morris, 1992, p. 156.

16 Dorothy Scott and Shurlee Swain, 2002, *Confronting Cruelty: Historical Perspectives on Child Protection in Australia.* Oxford, Oxford University Press, p. 71.

17 Jeffrey Weeks, 1989, *Sex, Politics and Society: The Regulation of Sexuality Since 1800*, 2nd edn. London, Longman, p. 48.

18 Anthony Wohl, 1978, "Sex and the single room: incest among the Victorian working classes", in Anthony Wohl (ed.), *The Victorian Family: Structure and Stresses.* London, Croom Helm, p. 204.

19 John D'Emilio and Estelle Freedman, 2002, "Family life and the regulation of deviance", in Kim Phillips and Barry Reay (eds), *Sexualities in History: A Reader.* New York, Routledge, p. 143.

20 Wohl, 1978, *op. cit.*, p. 205.

21 Weeks, 1989, *op. cit.*, p. 60.

22 Tim Hitchcock, 2002, "Redefining sex in eighteenth century England", in Kim Phillips and Barry Reay (eds), *Sexualities in History: A Reader.* New York, Routledge, p. 191.

23 Weeks, 1989, *op. cit.*, p. 48.

24 Lyn Finch, 1991, "The nineteenth century identification of incest as a working class crime: implications for analysis", in Penelope Hetherington (ed.), *Incest and the Australian Community: Australian Perspectives.* Osborne Park, WA, Optima Press, p. 19.

25 Carol Smart, 1992, "Disruptive bodies and unruly sex: the regulation of reproduction and sexuality in the nineteenth century", in Carol Smart (ed.), *Regulating Womanhood: Historical Essays on Marriage, Motherhood and Sexuality.* London, Routledge, p. 26.

26 J. Allen, 1990, *Sex and Secrets: Crimes Involving Australian Women Since 1880.* Melbourne, Oxford University Press, pp. 63 and 79.

27 J. Bavin-Mizzi, 1995, "Understandings of justice: Australian rape and carnal knowledge cases 1876–1924", in Diane Kirkby (ed.), *Sex, Power and Justice: Historical Perspectives on Law in Australia.* Oxford, Oxford University Press, pp. 19–32.

28 Finch, 1991, *op. cit.*, p. 20.

29 Finch, 1991, p. 28.

30 Smart, 1992, *op. cit.*, p. 25.

31 Phillipe Aries, 1989, "From immodesty to innocence", in Henry Jenkins (ed.), *The Children's Culture Reader.* New York, New York University Press, pp. 100–103.

32 D. Egan and G. Hawkes, 2009, "The problem with protection: or, why we need to move towards recognition and the sexual agency of children", *Continuum: Journal of Media & Cultural Studies*, 23(3), p. 448.

33 Egan and Hawkes, 2009, p. 390.

34 Kjersti Ericsson, 2005, "Child welfare as social defence against sexuality: a Norwegian example", in Elizabeth Bernstein and Laurie Schaffner (eds), *Regulating Sex: The Politics of Intimacy and Identity.* New York, Routledge, p. 130.

35 Ericsson, 2005, p. 131.

36 Egan and Hawkes, 2009, *op. cit.*, p. 455.

37 CAPTA, 1974, cited in Ericcson, 2005, *op. cit.*

38 Kerwin Kaye, 2005, "Sexual abuse victims and the wholesome family: feminist, psychological and state discourses", in Elizabeth Bernstein and Laurie Schaffner (eds), *Regulating Sex: The Politics of Intimacy and Identity.* New York, Routledge, p. 149.

39 Kaye, 2005, p. 157.

40 Kaye, 2005, p. 156.

41 Elizabeth Bernstein and Laurie Schaffner, 2005, "Regulating sex: an introduction", in Elizabeth Bernstein and Laurie Schaffner (eds), *Regulating Sex: The Politics of Intimacy and Identity.* New York, Routledge, p. xx.

42 Bernstein and Schaffner, 2005, p. xx.

43 Finch, 1991, *op. cit.*, p. 17.

44 Finch, 1991, p. 17. Scott and Swain, 2002, *op. cit.*, p. 171.

4 Pornography

1 New South Wales Supreme Court, 2008, *McEwen* v. *Simmons & ANOR*, NSWSC 1292, Reported Decision 73 NSWLR 10, 191 A Crim R 390. www.lawlink.nsw.go.au (accessed 29 September 2011).
2 Jack Healy, 2008, "Bart Simpson, child pornography and free speech", *The New York Times*, "The Lede: Blogging the *News* with Robert Mackey", 8 December. http://thelede. blogs.nytimes.com/2008/12/08/bart-simpson-child-pornography-and-free-speech (accessed 29 September 2011).
3 New South Wales Supreme Court, 2008, *op. cit.*
4 Neil M. Malamuth, Tamara Addison and Mary Koss, 2000, "Pornography and sexual aggression: are there reliable effects and can we understand them?", *Annual Review of Sex Research*, 11, 26–91; Susan M. Shaw, 1999, "Men's leisure and women's lives: the impact of pornography on women", *Leisure Studies*, 18(3), 197–212.
5 Michael Flood, 2007, "Exposure to pornography among youth in Australia", *Journal of Sociology*, 43(1), 45–60.
6 Stephen T. Holmes and Ronald M. Holmes, 2002, *Sex Crimes: Patterns and Behaviour*, 2nd edn. Thousand Oaks, CA, Sage.
7 Susanna Paasonen, Kaarina Nikunen and Laura Saarenmaa, 2007, "Pornification and the education of desire", in Susanna Paasonen, Kaarina Nikunen and Laura Saarenmaa (eds), *Pornification: Sex and Sexuality in Media Culture*. Oxford, Berg, p. 2.
8 Simon Hardy, 2008, "The pornography of reality", *Sexualities,* 11(1/2), 60.
9 Tim Hitchcock, 1997, *English Sexualities, 1700–1800*. London, Macmillan, p. 17.
10 Jeffrey Weeks, 1989, *Sex, Politics and Society: The Regulation of Sexuality Since 1800*, 2nd edn. London, Longman, p. 20.
11 Lyn Hunt, 1993a, "Introduction: obscenity and the origins of modernity, 1500–1800", in Lyn Hunt (ed.), *The Invention of Pornography*. New York, Zone Books, p. 10.
12 Barbara Sullivan, 1997, *The Politics of Sex: Prostitution and Pornography in Australia Since 1945*. Cambridge, Cambridge University Press, p. 32.
13 Weeks, 1989, *op. cit.*, p. 20.
14 Hitchcock, 1997, *op. cit.*
15 Hunt, 1993a, *op. cit.*, p. 10.
16 Hitchcock, 1997, *op. cit.*, p. 17.
17 Lyn Hunt, 1993b, "Pornography and the French Revolution", in Lyn Hunt (ed.), *The Invention of Pornography*. New York, Zone Books, pp. 301–39.
18 Hunt, 1993b, p. 306.
19 Robert Darnton, cited in Hunt, 1993a, *op. cit.*, p. 18.
20 Peter Wagner, 1988, *Eros Revived: Erotica of the Enlightenment in England and America*. London, Secker and Warburg.
21 Hunt, 1993a, *op. cit.*, p. 43.
22 Wagner, *op. cit.*, 1988.
23 Walter Kendrick, 1996, *The Secret Museum: Pornography in Modern Culture*. Berkeley, CA, University of California Press, p. 1.
24 Kendrick, 1996, p. 9.
25 Robert Darnton, 1996, *The Forbidden Best-Sellers of Pre-revolutionary France*. New York, W. W. Thornton & Company, p. 4.
26 Kendrick, 1996, *op. cit.*
27 Louis Barré, 1875–77, cited in Kendrick, 1996, p. 15.
28 Kendrick, 1996, p. 33.
29 Kendrick, 1996, p. 44.
30 Kendrick, 1996, p. 58; Hunt, 1993a, *op. cit.*
31 Kendrick, 1996, pp. 65–66.
32 Paul Findlen, 1993, "Humanism, politics and pornography in renaissance Italy", in Lyn Hunt (ed.), *The Invention of Pornography*. New York, Zone Books, p. 55.

33 Thomas Laqueur, 1990, *Making Sex: Body and Gender from the Greeks to Freud*. Boston, MA, Harvard University Press.
34 Gail Hawkes, 2004, *Sex and Pleasure in Western Culture*. Cambridge, Polity Press, p. 159.
35 Hawkes, 2004, p. 48.
36 Gail Hawkes and John Scott (eds), 2005, *Perspectives in Human Sexuality*. Melbourne, Oxford University Press, p. 8.
37 Hawkes and Scott, 2005, p. 8.
38 Frederick S. Lane, 2000, *Obscene Profits: The Entrepreneurs of Pornography in the Cyber Age*. New York: Routledge, p. 14.
39 Sharon Marcus, 1966, *The Other Victorians: A Study of Sexuality and Pornography in Mid-Nineteenth-Century England*. New York, Basic Books, p. 155.
40 Lucienne Frappier-Mazur, 1993, "Truth and the obscene word in eighteenth century French pornography", in Lyn Hunt (ed.), *The Invention of Pornography*. New York, Zone Books, p. 219.
41 Hunt, 1993a, *op. cit.*, p. 36.
42 Sullivan, 1997, *op. cit.*, p. 32–33.
43 Sullivan, 1997.
44 Lisa Z. Sigel, 2000, "Filth in the wrong people's hands: postcards and the expansion of pornography in Britain and the Atlantic world, 1880–1914", *Journal of Social History*, 33(4), 859–85.
45 Sigel, 2000, p. 860.
46 William Acton, 1857, cited in Marcus, 1966, *op. cit.*, pp. 13–14.
47 Danielle Egan and Gail Hawkes, 2009, "The problem with protection: or why we need to move towards recognition and the sexual agency of children", *Continuum: Journal of Media and Cultural Studies*, 23(3), 389–400.
48 Robert Darby, 2005, *A Surgical Temptation: The Demonization of the Foreskin and the Rise of Circumcision in Britain*. Chicago, IL, University of Chicago Press; Weeks, 1989, *op. cit.*
49 Darby, 2005, p. 270.
50 Marcus, 1966, *op. cit.*, p. 15.
51 Egan and Hawkes, 2009, *op. cit.*
52 Jane Arthurs, 2004, *Television and Sexuality: Regulation and the Politics of Taste*. New York: Open University Press, p. 21.
53 Gary Needham, 2008, "Scheduling normativity: television, the family, and queer temporality", in Glyn Davis and Gary Needham (eds), *Queer TV: Theories, Histories, Politics*, New York, Routledge.
54 Thomas Laqueur, 2003, *Solitary Sex: A Cultural History of Masturbation*. New York, Zone Books, p. 334.
55 Laqueur, 2003, p. 21.
56 Kendrick, 1996, *op. cit.*, p. 89.
57 Marcus, 1966, *op. cit.*
58 Edward B. Rosenman, 2003, *Unauthorized Pleasures: Accounts of Victorian Erotic Experience*. Ithaca, NY, Cornell University Press, p. 19.
59 As cited in Tim Hitchcock, 2002, "Redefining sex in eighteenth century England", in Kim M. Phillips and Barry Reay (eds), *Sexualities in History: A Reader*. New York, Routledge, p. 190.
60 Rosenman, 2003, *op. cit.*, p. 16.
61 Elizabeth Shorter, 1984, *A History of Women's Bodies*. Harmondsworth, Penguin, p. 12.
62 Hitchcock, 1997, *op. cit.*, p. 43.
63 Hitchcock, 1997, p. 43.
64 Felicity A. Nussbaum, 1995, "One part of womankind: prostitution and sexual geography in *Memoirs of a Woman of Pleasure*", *Differences*, 7(2), 16–40.
65 Nussbaum, 1995, p. 22.
66 Hitchcock, 1997, *op. cit.*, p. 45.
67 Laqueur, 1990, *op. cit.*

68 Hitchcock, 2002, *op. cit.*, p. 190.
69 Rosenman, 2003, *op. cit.*, p. 7.
70 Hitchcock, 2002, *op. cit.*, p. 191.
71 Laqueur, 2003, *op. cit.*, p. 155.
72 Laqueur, 2003, p. 151.
73 Weeks, 1989, *op. cit.*, p. 280.
74 Sullivan, 1997, *op. cit.*, p. 139.
75 Paul Wilson and Stephen Nugent, 1992, "Sexually explicit and violent media material: research and policy implications", in Paul Wilson (ed.), *Issues in Crime, Morality and Justice*. Canberra, Australian Institute of Criminology, p. 139.
76 Wilson and Nugent, 1992, pp. 139–41.
77 Wilson and Nugent, 1992, p. 140.
78 Paasonen, Nikunen and Saarenmaa, 2007, *op. cit.*, p. 1.

5 Out of place: the moral geography of sex and deviance

1 The following excerpts are from "The Subway", episode #313 of *Seinfeld*, written and produced by Larry Charles, originally aired on NBC, 8 January 1992. Transcript quoted from www.seinfeldscripts.com (accessed 29 September 2011).
2 Judith Halberstam, 2005, *In a Queer Time and Place: Transgender Bodies, Subcultural Lives*. New York, New York University Press.
3 Joel Feinberg, 1988. *The Moral Limits of the Criminal Law, Vol. 2*. Cambridge, Cambridge University Press.
4 Gill Valentine, 2004, *Public Space and the Culture of Childhood*. Aldershot, Ashgate Publishing, p. 8.
5 Valentine, 2004, p. 8.
6 Massey, cited in Valentine, 2004, p. 8.
7 Massey, cited in Valentine, 2004, p. 12.
8 Gary Needham, 2008, "Scheduling normality: television, the family and queer temporality", in Gary Needham and Glyn Davis (eds), *Queer TV: Theories, Histories, Politics*. New York, Routledge, pp. 143–58.
9 Chris Philo, 2005, "Sex, life, death, geography: fragmentary remarks inspired by Foucault's population geographies", *Population, Space and Place*, 11(4), 326.
10 Philo, 2005, p. 329.
11 Philo, 2005, p. 330.
12 Philo, 2005, p. 330.
13 Philo, 2005, p. 330.
14 M. Lisa Johnson, 2004, "Way more than a tag line: HBO, feminism, and the question of difference in popular culture," *The Scholar and the Feminist Online*, 3.1 (Fall), 1.
15 Johnson, 2005, p. 1.
16 Elizabeth Bernstein, 2007, *Temporarily Yours: Intimacy, Authenticity, and the Commerce of Sex*. Chicago, IL and London, University of Chicago Press.
17 Stephen Legg, 2005, "Foucault's population geographies: classifications, biopolitics and governmental spaces", *Population, Space and Place*, 11(4), 144.
18 David Bell and Jon Binnie, 2000, *The Sexual Citizen: Queer Politics and Beyond*. Cambridge, Polity Press.
19 Bell and Binnie, 2004.
20 Joel Feinberg, 1985, *The Moral Limits of the Criminal Law. Volume One: Offence to Others*. New York, Oxford University Press.
21 Feinberg, 1985, p. 10.
22 Feinberg, 1985, p. 1.
23 Feinberg, 1985, p. 17.
24 Feinberg, 1985, p. 17.
25 Feinberg, 1985, p. 17

26 Feinberg, 1985, p. 17.
27 Feinberg, 1985, p. 20.
28 Valentine 2004, *op. cit.*, pp. 1–2.
29 For example, see Rousseau's *Emile,* 1762.
30 Valentine, 2004, p. 3.
31 Anne Phoenix and Ann Woollett, 1991, cited in Valentine, 2004, p. 5.
32 Valentine, 2004, p. 6.
33 Valentine, 2004, p. 18.
34 Valentine, 2004, p. 18.
35 Valentine, 2004, p. 20.
36 John Holt, 1974, *Escape from Childhood – The Needs and Rights of Children.* New York, E.P. Dutton and Co., p. 222.
37 Cindi Katz, 2006, "Power, space and terror: social reproduction and the public environment", in Setha Low and Neil Smith (eds), *The Politics of Public Space.* New York, Routledge, p. 3.
38 Valentine, 2004, *op. cit.*, p. 23.
39 Valentine, 2004, pp. 69–74.
40 Valentine, 2004, p. 83.
41 Valentine, 2004, p. 84.
42 Valentine, 2004, p. 89.
43 Marcel Henaff and Tracey B. Strong (eds), 2001 *Public Space and Democracy.* Minneapolis, MN, University of Minnesota Press.
44 Johnson, 2005, *op. cit.*, p. 10.
45 Sharon Hayes and Matthew Ball, 2009, "Queering cyberspace: fan fiction communities as spaces for expressing and exploring sexuality", in Burkhard Scherer (ed.), *Queering Paradigms.* Oxford, Peter Lang.
46 Clare Madge and Henrietta O'Connor, 2005, "Mothers in the making? Exploring liminality in cyber/space", *Transactions of the Institute of British Geographers,* 301, 83–97.

6 Sex offending

1 Liza Kappelle and Andrea Hayward, 2007, "Sofia's killer jailed for life over toilet murder", www.news.com.au/sofias-killer-jailed-for-life-over-toilet-murder/story-e6frfkp9-1111114822414 (accessed 29 September 2011).
2 Supreme Court of Western Australia, 2007, *Arthurs v. The State of Western Australia,* WASC 182, 31 July. www.austlii.edu.au/cgi-bin/sinodisp/au/cases/wa/WASC/2007/182.html (accessed 29 September 2011).
3 Terry Thomas, 2005, *Sex Crime: Sex Offending and Society*, 2nd edn. London, Willan Publishing, p. 18.
4 Thomas, 2005, p. 1.
5 James F. Quinn, Carla R. Forsyth and Craig Mullen-Quinn, 2004, "Societal reactions to sex offenders: a review of the origins and results of the myths surrounding their crimes and treatment amenability", *Deviant Behaviour,* 25(3), 219.
6 Steve Garton, 2004, *Histories of Sexuality: Antiquity to Sexual Revolution.* London, Equinox.
7 Gail Hawkes and John Scott (eds), 2005, *Perspectives in Human Sexuality.* Melbourne, Oxford University Press, p. 8.
8 William Naphy, 2002, *Sex Crimes: From Renaissance to Enlightenment.* Stroud, UK, Tempus Publishing, p. 9.
9 Steven R. Morrison, 2007, "Creating sex offender registries: the religious right and the failure to protect society's vulnerable", *American Journal of Criminal Law,* 35(1), 38.
10 Tim Hitchcock, 1997, *English Sexualities 1700–1800.* London, Macmillan, p. 5.
11 Hitchcock, 1997, p. 5.
12 Gail Hawkes, 2004, *Sex and Pleasure in Western Culture.* Cambridge, Polity Press, p. 66.
13 Hitchcock, 1997, p. 5.

14 Tim Hitchcock, 2002, "Redefining sex in eighteenth century England", in Kim Phillips and Barry Reay (eds), *Sexualities in History: A Reader*. New York, Routledge, p. 191.
15 Jeffrey Weeks, 1989, *Sex, Politics and Society*, 2nd edn. London, Longman.
16 Hitchcock, 1997, *op. cit.*, p. 99.
17 Laura Agustin, 1988, *Sex at the Margins*. London, Zed Books.
18 William Mayhew, 1851, cited in Agustin, 1988, p. 99.
19 Hitchcock, 1997, *op. cit.*, p. 99.
20 Hitchcock, 1997, p. 100.
21 Hitchcock, 1997, p. 100.
22 Hitchcock, 1997, p. 15.
23 Hitchcock, 1997, p. 101.
24 Thomas, 2005, *op. cit.*, p. 40.
25 Hawkes, 2004, *op. cit.*, p. 91.
26 Naphy, 2002, *op. cit.*, pp. 84–85.
27 John D'Emilio and Estelle Freedman, 2002, "Family Life and the Regulation of Deviance", in Kim Phillips and Barry Reay (eds), *Sexualities in History: A Reader*. New York, Routledge, p. 141.
28 Marjorie McIntosh, 1998, *Controlling Misbehaviour in England, 1370–1600*. Cambridge, Cambridge University Press.
29 Philip Jenkins, 1998, *Moral Panic: Changing Concepts of the Child Molester in Modern America*. New Haven, CT, Yale University Press, p. 26.
30 Michel Foucault, 1976, *The History of Sexuality: An Introduction*. London, Penguin.
31 Kim Phillips and Barry Reay, 2002, "Introduction", in Phillips and Reay, *op. cit.*, p. 13.
32 Mona Lynch, 2002, "Pedophiles and cyber-predators as contaminating forces: the language of disgust, pollution, and boundary invasions in federal debates on sex offender legislation", *Law & Social Inquiry*, 27, 557.
33 Jenkins, 1998, *op. cit.*, p. 22.
34 Jenkins, 1998, p. 12.
35 Morrison, 2007, *op. cit.*, 44–45.
36 Jenkins, 1998, *op. cit.*, p. 21.
37 Laura J. Zilney and Lisa A. Zilney, 2009, *Perverts and Predators: The Making of Sexual Offending Laws*. Lanham, MD, Rowman & Littlefield, pp. 66–67.
38 Estelle B. Freedman, 1987, "'Uncontrolled desires': the response to the sexual psychopath, 1920–60", *Journal of American History*, 74(1), 84.
39 Thomas, 2005, *op. cit.*, p. 15.
40 Foucault, 1976, *op. cit.*, p. 43.
41 Michael Petrunik, 2003, "The hare and the tortoise: dangerousness and sex offender policy in the United States and Canada", *Canadian Journal of Criminology and Criminal Justice*, 43(1), 43.
42 Robert Castel, 1991, "From dangerousness to risk", in Graeme Burchell, Colin Gordon and Peter Miller (eds), *The Foucault Effect: Studies in Governmentality*. London, Harvester, p. 283.
43 Gordon Tait, 2000, *Youth, Sex and Government*. Peter Lang, New York, p. 115.
44 David McCallum, 2001, *Personality and Dangerousness*. Cambridge, Cambridge University Press, p. 34.
45 Tait, 2000, *op. cit.*, p. 114.
46 Thomas, 2005, *op. cit.*, p. 121.
47 Petrunik, 2003, *op. cit.*, p. 44.
48 Thomas, 2005, pp. 156–58.
49 Michel Foucault, 1961, *Madness and Civilization: A History if Insanity in the Age of Reason*. London, Routledge, p. 55.
50 Thomas, 2005, pp. 220–24.
51 Australian Institute of Criminology, 2007, *Is Notification of Sex Offenders in Local Communities Effective?* Canberra, AIC; Bob E. Vásquez, Sean Maddan and Jeffrey

T. Walker, 2008, "The influence of sex offender registration and notification laws in the United States: a time-series analysis", *Crime and Delinquency*, 54(2), 175–92.

52 Michelle L. Meloy, Yustina Saleh and Nancy Wolff, 2007, "Sex offender laws in America: can panic-driven legislation ever create safer societies?", *Criminal Justice Studies*, 20(4), 438.

53 Kevin Brown, Jon W. Spencer and Jo Deakin, 2007, "The reintegration of sex offenders: barriers and opportunities for employment", *Howard Journal of Criminal Justice*, 46(1), 32–42.

54 Petrunik, 2003, *op. cit.*, p. 44.

55 Petrunik, 2003, p. 43.

56 Thomas, 2005, *op. cit.*, p. 4.

57 Paul A. Zandbergen   and Timothy C. Hart cited in Jill S. Levenson, 2008, "Collateral consequences of sex offender residence restrictions", *Criminal Justice Studies*, 21(2), p. 155.

58 Jill S. Levenson, Kristen Zgoba and Richard Tewksbury, 2007, "Sex offender residence restrictions: sensible crime policy or flawed logic?", *Federal Probation*, 71(3), 2–9.

59 Julian C. Roberts, Loretta J. Stalans, David Indermaur and Michael Hough, 2003, *Penal Populism and Public Opinion: Lessons from Five Countries.* Oxford, Oxford University Press.

60 Roberts, Stalans, Indermaur and Hough, 2003, p. 141.

7 Sexuality

1 See, for example, "*Belle de Jour:* Diary of a London CallGirl", http://belledejour-uk. blogspot.com; "Girl With a One-track Mind", http://girlwithaonetrackmind.blogspot. com; "PurrVersatility", http://purrversatility.blogspot.com; "Bitchy Jones's Diary", http://bitchyjones.wordpress.com (all accessed 29 September 2011).

2 "Queer theory" is the name given to a branch of scholarly literature that theorizes sexuality, especially non-heterosexualities, and gender deviance.

3 Elzabeth Bernstein and Laurie Schaffer, 2005, *Regulating Sex: The Politics of Intimacy and Identity*, New York, Routledge.

4 http://girlwithaonetrackmind.blogspot.com (accessed 29 September 2011).

5 http://purrversatility.blogspot.com (accessed 29 September 2011).

6 The papers in this seminar were organized by Lisa Downing. The following two papers are forthcoming in a special issue of *Psychology and Sexuality*, 3(1), 2012, on sex blogging and feminism, edited by Lisa Downing, Meg Barker and Feona Attwood: Kaye Mitchell, "Raunch vs prude: contemporary sex blogs and erotic memoirs by women"; Meg Barker and Ros Gill, "Sexual subjectification and 'Bitchy Jones's Diary'".

7 http://belledejour-uk.blogspot.com (accessed 29 September 2011).

8 http://bitchyjones.wordpress.com (accessed 29 September 2011).

9 Where a "femdom" is a female dominatrix and a "prodom" is a professional dominatrix.

10 Susie Bright, 1990, *Susie Sexpert's Lesbian Sex World.* Pittsburgh, PA, Cleis Press; Ellen Willis, 1992, "Feminism, moralism, and pornography", in Ellen Willis, *Beginning to See the Light: Sex, Hope, and Rock-and-Roll.* Hanover, NH, Wesleyan University Press; D. Leidholdt and J. Raymond, 1990, *The Sexual Liberals and the Attack on Feminism.* Oxford, Pergamon Press; Liz Morrish and Helen Sauntson, 2007, *New Perspectives on Language and Sexual Identity.* Houndmills, UK, Palgrave Macmillan.

11 Katy Perry, Dr Luke, Max Martin and Cathy Dennis, 2008, *I Kissed a Girl.* Capitol Music.

12 www.tatugirls.com (accessed 29 September 2011).

13 www.urbandictionary.com/define.php?term=Barsexual (accessed 29 September 2011).

14 The term "queer", while once a derogative term, more recently has been widely adopted among non-heteronormative individuals and theoretical scholars to denote sexual and/or gender difference.

15 M. Kirby, 2010, "Unequal Laws Affecting Homosexual Citizens in Queensland", www. queerradio.org/Hon_Michael_Kirby_3rdFebruary2010.pdf (accessed 29 September 2011).

16 Kirby, 2010.

17 USLegal, Inc., 2010, http://uslegal.com (accessed 29 September 2011).

18 Chuck Stewart, 2001, *Homosexuality and the Law: A Dictionary.* Santa Barbara, CA, ABC-Clio.

19 Wayne Morrison (ed.), 2001, *Commentaries on the Laws of England.* London, Cavendish Publishing.

20 Karl Menninger, 1964, *The Wolfenden Report.* Lancer Books.

21 *Toonen* v. *Australia,* 1972.

22 David Smith, 2010, "UN's human rights chief urges Uganda to scrap anti-gay legislation", *The Guardian,* 15 January, www.guardian.co.uk/world/2010/jan/15/un-human-rights-uganda-gay-legislation (accessed 29 September 2011).

23 Foucault, 1976.

24 H. Dreyfus and P. Rabinow, 1982, *Michel Foucault: Beyond Structuralism and Hermeneutics.* Brighton, UK, Harvester Press.

25 Michel Foucault, 1998, *The Will to Knowledge: The History of Sexuality Volume 1.* London, Penguin.

26 David Halperin, 1995, *Saint Foucault: Towards a Gay Hagiography.* Oxford, Oxford University Press.

27 Eve Kosofsky Sedgwick, 1990, *Epistemology of the Closet.* Berkeley, CA, University of California Press.

28 Sedgwick, 1990.

29 S. Hayes and M. Ball, 2009, "Queering cyberspace: fan fiction communities as spaces for expressing and exploring sexuality", in Burkhard Scherer (ed.), *Queering Paradigms.* Oxford, Peter Lang.

30 Hayes and Ball, 2009.

31 The currently accepted term for such individuals is "transgender".

32 HRC, 2007, *Same Sex: Same Entitlements.* Canberra, Human Rights Commission.

33 Haroon Siddique, 2009, "Boyzone singer Stephen Gately dies on holiday", *The Guardian,* 11 October, www.guardian.co.uk/music/2009/oct/11/stephen-gately-death-majorca (accessed 29 September 2011).

34 Siddique, 2009.

35 Roy Greenslade, 2009, "Mail columnist provides homophobia storm over Stephen Gately's death", *The Guardian,* 16 October, www.guardian.co.uk/media/greenslade/2009/oct/16/dailymail-stephen-gately (accessed 29 September 2011).

36 Greenslade, 2009.

37 Charlie Brooker, 2009, "Why there was nothing 'human' about Jan Moir's column on the death of Stephen Gately", *The Guardian,* 16 October, www.guardian.co.uk/commentisfree/2009/oct/16/stephen-gately-jan-moir (accessed 29 September 2011).

38 Adam Fresco, 2009, "Murder inquiry as homophobic attack man Ian Baynham dies", *Times Online,* 15 October, www.timesonline.co.uk/tol/news/uk/crime/article6874257.ece (accessed 29 September 2011).

39 Jessica Green, 2009, "Convictions for homophobic hate crime increase", *Pink News,* 9 December, www.pinknews.co.uk/2009/12/18/convictions-for-homophobic-hate-crime-increase (accessed 29 September 2011).

40 See Morrish and Sauntson, 2007, *op. cit.,* for an excellent discussion of homosexual shame. Our thanks to Liz Morrish for discussions of shame.

41 Judith Butler, 1993, *Bodies that Matter: On the Discursive Limits of Sex.* New York, Routledge, p. 2.

42 Eve Kosofsky Sedgwick, cited in Morrish and Sauntson, 2007, *op. cit.,* p. 92.

8 Out of context: the moral economy of sex and harm

1 Emine Saner, 2007, "Wrong call", *The Guardian,* 20 September (Comment 1), p. 1.

2 Saner, 2007, p. 1.

3 Daubney, 2007, "Wrong call", *The Guardian,* 20 September (Comment 3), p. 3.

4 Daubney, 2007, p. 3.
5 Saner, 2007, p. 2.
6 Mitchell, 2007, "Wrong call", *The Guardian*, 20 September (Comment 5), p. 4.
7 Hedley, 2007, "Wrong call", *The Guardian*, 20 September (Comment 4), p. 4.
8 Daubney, 2007, p. 3.
9 Hedley, 2007, "Wrong call", *The Guardian*, 20 September (Comment 2), p. 2.
10 Hedley, 2007, p. 2.
11 Michael L. Rekart, 2005, "Sex-work harm reduction", *The Lancet*, 366, December 17/24/31.
12 CATWA, 2009, www.catwa.org.au (accessed 29 September 2011).
13 CATWA, 2009.
14 CATWA, 2009.
15 Joel Feinberg, 1985, *The Moral Limits of the Criminal Law, Vol. 1*, Oxford, Oxford University Press, p. 221.
16 Feinberg, 1985, p. 223.
17 Rekart, 2005, *op. cit.*, p. 366.
18 Rekart, 2005.
19 Rekart, 2005.
20 Scott A. Lucas, 2010, "Sex", *The Gender Ads Project*. www.ltcconline.net/lukas/gender/pages/sex.htm (accessed 29 September 2011).
21 Joel Feinberg, 1988, *The Moral Limits of the Criminal Law, Vol. 2*, Oxford, Oxford University Press.
22 Feinberg, 1988.
23 Feinberg, 1988.
24 Feinberg, 1988, pp. 11–12.
25 Feinberg, 1985, *op. cit.*, p. 10.
26 Belle De Jour and Anonymous, 2008, *Secret Diary of a Call Girl*. New York: Grand Central Publishing, p. 39; Catharine Lumby, 1997, *Bad Girls: The Media, Sex & Feminism in the 90s*. St Leonards, Australia, Allen & Unwin.
27 Catharine Lumby, 1997, "Girls and the new media," *Meanjin*, Vol. 56(1), p. 110.
28 Natasha Walters, for example, makes this point in her 2010 book *Living Dolls: The Return of Sexism*. London, Virago Press.
29 Ariel Levy, 2005, *Female Chauvinist Pigs: Women and the Rise of Raunch Culture*, New York, Free Press.
30 Nina Funnell, 2009, "Don't patronise ladies who raunch", *REVLEFT*, 25 February. www.revleft.com/vb/group.php?do=discuss&gmid=20131 (accessed 29 September 2011).
31 Funnell, 2009.
32 Lumby, 1997, *op. cit.*
33 Lumby, Catharine, 2009, "Manhunters: sex trips for girls", www.sbs.com.au/blogarticle/113377/Manhunters-Sex-Trips-for-Girls-br/blog/Catharine-Lumby-br (accessed 29 September 2011).

9 Sexual commerce

1 "Eros Guide San Francisco", www.eros-sf.com (accessed 29 September 2011).
2 Elizabeth Bernstein, 2007, *Temporarily Yours: Intimacy, Authenticity and the Commerce of Sex*. Chicago, IL and London, University of Chicago Press, p. 71.
3 Benjamin Edelman, 2009 "Red light states: who buys online adult entertainment?", *Journal of Economic Perspectives*, 23(1), 209–20.
4 Bernstein, 2007, *op. cit.*, p. 13.
5 Jeffrey Weeks, 1989, *Sex, Politics and Society: The Regulation of Sexuality Since 1800*, 2nd edn. London and New York, Longman, p. 29.
6 Weeks, 1989, p. 32.
7 Judith Walkowitz, 1988, *Prostitution and Victorian Society: Women, Class and the State*. Cambridge, Cambridge University Press, p. 4.

8 Walkowitz, 1988, p. 34.

9 Laura Maria Agustin, 1988, *Sex at the Margins: Migration, Labour and Markets and the Rescue Industry*. London and New York, Zed Books.

10 Walkowitz, 1988, p. 78.

11 Agustin, 1988.

12 Walkowitz, 1988.

13 Agustin, 1988, p. 14.

14 Agustin, 1988.

15 Laura Maria Agustin, 2005, "New research directions: the cultural study of commercial sex", *Sexualities*, 8(5), 618 and 622.

16 Murray Cowper, cited in Ronald Weitzer, 2009, "Legalizing prostitution: morality politics in Western Australia", *British Journal of Criminology*, 48(1), 7.

17 Janice Raymond, 2003, "Ten reasons for not legalizing prostitution and a legal response to the demand for prostitution", *Journal of Trauma Practice*, 2, 315–32.

18 Melissa Farley, 2005, "Prostitution harms women even if indoors", *Violence Against Women*, 11(7), 950–64; Jody Raphael and Deborah Shapiro, 2005, "Reply to Weitzer", *Violence Against Women*, 11(7), 965–70.

19 Ine Vanwesenbeeck, 2001, "Another decade of social scientific work on sex work: a review of research 1990–2000", *Annual Review of Sex Research*, 12, 242–89.

20 Vanwesenbeeck, 2001.

21 Ronald Weitzer, 2005, "New directions in research on prostitution", *Crime, Law and Social Change*, 43: 211–35.

22 Vanwesenbeeck, 2001, p. 263.

23 Cited in Agustin, 1988, *op. cit.*, p. 99.

24 Agustin, 1988, p. 100.

25 Agustin 1988, p. 10.

26 William Mayhew, 1851, cited in Agustin, 1988.

27 Hilary Golder and Judith Allen, 1979, "Prostitution in New South Wales 1870–1932: restructuring an industry", *Refractory Girl*, December 1979, p. 21.

28 Golder and Allen, 1979, p. 20.

29 Golder and Allen, 1979, p. 20.

30 Feona Attwood, 2007, "No money shot? Commerce, pornography and new sex taste cultures", *Sexualities*, 10(4), 441–56.

31 Attwood, 2007, p. 443.

32 Attwood, 2007, p. 444.

33 Attwood, 2007, p. 444.

34 Gail Hawkes, 2004, *Sex and Pleasure in Western Culture*, Polity Press, Cambridge, p. 8.

35 Pauline Chiou, 2009, "Girls sell sex in Hong Kong to earn shopping money", CNN. com/asia, 13 October, http://edition.cnn.com/2009/WORLD/asiapcf/09/24/hongkong. teenage.prostitution (all accessed 29 September 2011).

36 Clare Shipman and Cole Kazdin, 2009, "Oral sex as the new goodnight kiss", *ABC Good Morning America*, 28 May, abcnews.go.com (accessed 29 September 2011).

37 Norbert Elias, cited in Gail Hawkes, 2004, *Sex and Pleasure in Western Culture*. Cambridge, Polity Press, pp. 7–8.

38 Golder and Allen, 1979, *op. cit.*, p. 18.

39 Crime and Misconduct Commission, 2004, *Regulating Prostitution: An Evaluation of the Prostitution Act 1999 (Qld)*. Brisbane, Crime and Misconduct Commission, p. 32.

40 Belinda Carpenter, 2004, "Good prostitutes and bad prostitutes: some unintended consequences of governmental regulation", in Richard Hill and Gordon Tait (eds), *Hard Lessons: critical reflections on crime control in late modernity*, Ashgate, UK.

41 Teela Sanders, 2006, "Behind the personal ads: the indoor sex markets in Britain", in Rosie Campbell and Maggie O'Neill (eds), *Sex Work Now*. Cullompton, UK, Willan Publishing.

42 Sanders, 2006, p. 108.

43 Sanders, 2006, p. 109.
44 Bernstein, 2007, *op. cit.*, p.93.
45 Sanders, 2006, p. 108.
46 Sanders 2006, p. 110
47 Bernstein, 2007, p. 73.
48 Bernstein, 2007, p. 74.
49 Hawkes, 2004, *op. cit.*, p. 6.
50 Hawkes, 2004, p. 14.
51 Bernstein, 2007.
52 Bernstein, 2007, p. 6.
53 Hawkes, 2004, p. 14.
54 Bernstein, 2007, p. 110.
55 Hawkes, 2004, p. 12.
56 Hawkes, 2004, p. 16
57 Hawkes, 2004, p. 17.
58 Bernstein, 2007.
59 Cited in Bernstein, 2007, p. 121.
60 Cited in Bernstein, 2007, p. 113.
61 Monica Prasad, 1999, "The morality of market exchange: love, money, and contractual justice", *Sociological Perspectives*, 42(2), p. 206.

10 Sex trafficking

1 Kerry Carrington and Jane Hearn, 2003, "Trafficking and the Sex Industry: From Impunity to Protection", *Current Issues Brief* No. 28. Canberra, Parliamentary Library, Parliament of Australia, www.aph.gov.au/library/pubs (accessed 29 September 2011).
2 Carrington and Hearn, 2003.
3 Jyoti Sanghera, 2005, "Unpacking the trafficking discourse", in Kamala Kempadoo (ed.), *Trafficking and Prostitution Reconsidered: New Perspectives on Migration, Sex Work and Human Rights*. London, Paradigm, p. 6.
4 Kamala Kempadoo, 2005, "From moral panic to global justice: changing perspectives on trafficking", in Kamala Kempadoo (ed.), *Trafficking and Prostitution Reconsidered: New Perspectives on Migration, Sex Work and Human Rights*. London, Paradigm.
5 www2.ohchr.org/english/law/protocoltraffic.htm (accessed 29 September 2011).
6 Fiona David, 2008, "Trafficking of Women for Sexual Purposes", *Research and Public Policy Series* No. 95. Canberra, Australian Institute of Criminology, p. 3.
7 CATW, www.catwinternational.org (accessed 29 September 2011).
8 GAATW, www.gaatw.org (accessed 29 September 2011).
9 Kristina Touzenis, 2010, *Trafficking in Human Beings: Human Rights and Trans-National Criminal Law, Developments in Law and Practices*. Paris, UNESCO.
10 Judy Putt, 2007, "Human trafficking to Australia: a research challenge", *Trends and Issues in Crime and Criminal Justice*, No. 338. Canberra, Australian Institute of Criminology.
11 David, 2008, *op. cit.*
12 Toni Makkai, 2004, "What do we know? Improving the evidence base on trafficking inhuman beings in the Asia–Pacific region", *Development Bulletin*, 66, 36–42.
13 www.state.gov/g/tip/rls/tiprpt (accessed 29 September 2011).
14 Putt, 2007, *op. cit.*
15 Wendy Chapkis, 2005, "Soft glove, punishing fist: the Trafficking Victims Protection Act of 2000", in E. Bernstein and L. Schaffer (eds), *Regulating Sex: The Politics of Intimacy and Identity*. New York, Routledge, p. 54.
16 Putt, 2007, *op. cit.*
17 US GOA, 2006, *Human Trafficking: Better Data, Strategy, and Reporting Needed to Enhance U.S. Antitrafficking Efforts Abroad*. Washington, DC, US Government Accountability Office, www.gao.gov/new.items/d06825.pdf (accessed 29 September 2011).

18 Carrington and Hearn, 2003, *op. cit.*
19 Putt, 2007, *op. cit.*
20 Makkai, 2004, *op. cit.*
21 David, 2008, *op. cit.*
22 Kempadoo, 2005, *op. cit.*, p. xiii.
23 Jo Doezema, 1998, "Forced to choose: beyond the voluntary vs forced prostitution dichotomy", in Kamala Kempadoo and Jo Doezema (eds), *Global Sex Workers: Rights, Resistance and Redefinition*. New York, Routledge, p. 36.
24 Sheila Jeffreys, 1997, *The Idea of Prostitution*. Melbourne, Spinifex Press, p. 10.
25 Jeffreys, 1997, p. 10.
26 Judith Walkowitz, 1988, *Prostitution and Victorian Society: Women, Class and the State*. Cambridge, Cambridge University Press.
27 Jo Doezema, 2000, "Loose women or lost women? The re-emergence of the myth of white slavery in contemporary discourses of trafficking in women", *Gender Issues*, winter, 28.
28 Doezema, 2000, p. 29.
29 Walkowitz, 1988, *op. cit.*, p. 247.
30 Walkowitz, 1988, p. 247.
31 Kempadoo, 2005, *op. cit.*, p. x.
32 Walkowitz, 1988, *op. cit.*
33 League of Nations, 1921, cited in Jeffreys, 1997, *op. cit.*, p. 10.
34 Jeffreys, 1997, p. 15.
35 League of Nations 1927, cited in Jeffreys, 1997, p. 15.
36 Jeffreys, 1997, p. 16.
37 League of Nations, 1927, cited in Jeffreys, 1997, p. 16.
38 Barbara Sullivan, 2003, "Trafficking in women", *International Feminist Journal of Politics*, 5(1), 68.
39 Sullivan, 2003, p. 69.
40 Penelope Saunders, 2009, "Migrant sex workers exposed! The creation of trafficking policy in Australia", unpublished research paper.
41 Donna Hughes, 2001, "The Natasha trade: transnational sex trafficking", *National Institute of Justice Journal*, January, 11.
42 Chapkis, 2005, *op. cit.*, p. 55.
43 Hughes, 2001, p. 12.
44 Kathleen Maltzhan, 2004, *Combating Trafficking in Women: Where To Now?* Brisbane, Australia, The Brisbane Institute.
45 Cited in Doezema, 1998, *op. cit.*, p. 44.
46 Doezema, 2000, *op. cit.*, p. 34.
47 Alison Murray, 1998, "Debt bondage and trafficking: don't believe the hype", in Kamala Kempadoo and Jo Doezema (eds), *Global Sex Workers: Rights, Resistance and Redefinition*. New York, Routledge, p. 57.
48 Carrington and Hearn, 2003, *op. cit.*, p. 4.
49 Saunders, 2009, *op. cit.*
50 Saunders, 2009.
51 Doezema, 2000, *op. cit.*, p. 43.
52 Doezema, 1998, *op. cit.*, p. 45.
53 Chapkis, 2005, *op. cit.*, p. 58.
54 Doezema, 2000, p. 47.
55 Laura Agustin, 2008, *Sex at the Margins: Migration, Labour Markets and the Rescue Industry*. London and New York: Zed Books, p. 16.
56 Agustin, 2008, p. 19.
57 Kamala Kempadoo, 1998, "Introduction to globalising sex workers' rights", in Kamala Kempadoo and Jo Doezema (eds), *Global Sex Workers: Rights, Resistance and Redefinition*. New York, Routledge, p. 15.

58 Ratna Kapur, 2005, "Cross border movements and the law: renegotiating the boundaries of difference", in Kamala Kempadoo (ed.), *Trafficking and Prostitution Reconsidered: New Perspectives on Migration, Sex Work and Human Rights*. London, Paradigm, p. 27.
59 Murray, 1998, *op. cit.*, p. 59.
60 Kempadoo, 1998, *op. cit.*, p. 14.
61 Kempadoo, 1998, p. 15.
62 David, 2008, *op. cit.*, p. 30.
63 Agustin, 2008, *op. cit.*
64 Chapkis, 2005, *op. cit.*
65 Murray, 1998, *op. cit.*
66 Agustin, 2008, *op. cit.*, p. 33.
67 Agustin, 2008, p. 25.
68 Agustin, 2008, p. 27.
69 Agustin, 2008, p. 21.
70 Agustin, 2008.
71 Kempadoo, 1998, p. 17.
72 Marjan Wijers, 1998, "Women, labour and migration: the position of trafficking women and strategies for support", in Kamala Kempadoo and Jo Doezema (eds), *Global Sex Workers: Rights, Resistance and Redefinition*. New York, Routledge, p. 72.
73 Agustin, 2008, *op. cit.*, p. 27.
74 Agustin, 2008, p. 28.
75 Murray, 1998, *op. cit.*, pp. 57–8.
76 Murray, 1998, p. 58.
77 Doezema, 1998, p. 42.
78 Kempadoo, 1998, *op. cit.*, p. 11.
79 Kempadoo, 2005, *op. cit.*, p. xvii.
80 Kapur, 2005, *op. cit.*, p. 28.
81 Kempadoo, 2005, p. xvi.
82 Cited in Agustin, 2008, *op. cit.*, p. 31.
83 Cited in Agustin, 2008, p. 32.
84 Cited in Agustin, 2008, p. 33.
85 Cited in Agustin, 2008, p. 46.
86 Kempadoo, 2005, p. xxiv.

11 Conclusion

1 James Kincaid, 1998, *Erotic Innocence: The Culture of Child Molesting*, Durham, NC, Duke University Press.
2 Kincaid, 1998.

INDEX